THE WICKED WIT OF
JOHN F. KENNEDY

THE
WICKED WIT
OF
JOHN F.
KENNEDY

Compiled and introduced by
Christina Koning

MICHAEL O'MARA BOOKS LIMITED

First published in Great Britain in 2003 by
Michael O'Mara Books Limited
9 Lion Yard, Tremadoc Road
London SW4 7NQ

Copyright © 2003 by Michael O'Mara Books Ltd

A CIP catalogue record for this book
is available from the British Library

ISBN 1-84317-057-4

1 3 5 7 9 10 8 6 4 2

Photograph credits: Cecil Stoughton, White House/John
Fitzgerald Kennedy Library, Boston – pp. 1, 25, 83, 109, 119, 129,
151, 157, 162; John Fitzgerald Kennedy Library, Boston – pp. 15, 143;
Abbie Rowe, National Park Service/John Fitzgerald Kennedy
Library, Boston – p. 49; US Department of State/John Fitzgerald
Kennedy Library, Boston – p. 135; Robert Knudsen, White
House/John Fitzgerald Kennedy Library, Boston – p. 147.

Designed and typeset by Martin Bristow

Printed and bound in Finland
by WS Bookwell, Juva

Contents

Introduction

JOHN FITZGERALD KENNEDY was born on 29 May
1917 at his parents' home at 83 Beals Street, Brook-
line, Massachusetts. The second child of a self-made
Boston businessman, Joseph Patrick Kennedy and his
wife, Rose Fitzgerald Kennedy, the young JFK was a
delicate child, whose childhood passed in a succession of ailments and set the pattern for a lifelong
battle with ill-health. In spite of this, John Fitzgerald
– or 'Jack' as he was universally known – was a cheer-
ful child, much given to pranks and word-play, even
at an early age. In old age, his mother Rose recalled
him as 'a very active, very lively elf, full of energy
when he wasn't ill, and full of charm and imagination.' Some of his childhood witticisms appealed to
her so much that she jotted them down in her diary.
'Jack did not care so much for wishing for a happy
death,' she noted of the five-year-old (who was pre-
sumably responding to a remark by his devoutly
Catholic mother), 'but thought he would like to wish
for two dogs.' The wit, like the poor health, was to
endure.

His childhood was privileged. By the early 1920s,
Joseph Kennedy, the scion of Irish immigrants to

whose humble beginnings JFK was later to refer with pride, had established the considerable fortune which was to provide his wife and ten children with a spacious and elegant lifestyle, and which was later to launch the political careers of three of his sons. The family's summer retreat at Hyannis Port, on Long Island, was to remain a refuge for the whole 'Kennedy clan' during and after the turbulent years of JFK's presidency. Jack himself was sent to a succession of expensive private schools, eventually graduating from Choate in 1935 as the student 'most likely to succeed' of his peers. A spell at the London School of Economics followed, before JFK began his studies at Harvard University in 1936. Here, he threw himself with gusto into the social and sporting life of the university, earning himself the nickname 'Playboy', and gaining a reputation as a ladies' man which was to follow him throughout his life.

Aged twenty-one, Jack Kennedy received a $1,000,000 trust fund from his father, which enabled him to spend part of the next two years (1938–9) travelling in Europe, and to see for himself the spread of fascism in Italy and Germany – an experience which was to shape his political credo. As secretary to his father, recently appointed Ambassador to Great Britain, JFK also revisited London, and later made brief visits to Turkey, Poland and Russia. In his subsequent political career, these experiences were to give authority to JFK's pronouncements on world affairs, and to influence his views – particularly on the rise of Communism. Graduating *cum laude* from Harvard in 1940, with a Bachelor of Science degree,

JFK published his honours thesis – a study of the
Munich crisis ('Why England Slept') – which was to
become a bestseller. He then enrolled at Stanford
Business School, but withdrew after six months in
order to travel in South America. In September of
1941, after America had entered the Second World
War, JFK enlisted in the US Navy, rising from ensign
to lieutenant in the course of the next four years, and
gaining command of a PT-109 torpedo boat.

JFK's war record was distinguished. On 2 August
1943, his boat was rammed by a Japanese destroyer in
the South Pacific, and sank, four miles off the coast
of Olasana Island. Followed by other members of his
crew, JFK swam to shore from the burning boat, towing an injured crew-man by the strap of his life
jacket, which he held in his teeth – a feat for which
he won the Purple Heart. 'His courage, endurance
and excellent leadership contributed to the saving of
several lives and was in keeping with the traditions of
the United States Naval Service,' read the citation.
The following year, Jack's elder brother Joseph
Kennedy Jr was killed in action, when his aircraft was
shot down over Europe. Both these events were to
have a formative effect on JFK's attitude towards war,
and his later support for the principle of global disar-
mament. As a result of his ordeal in the South
Pacific, the serious back problem from which JFK
had suffered for several years worsened, and he was
honourably discharged from the Navy in 1945.

After a brief period working as a journalist,
covering the United Nations conference in San
Francisco, JFK launched his political career, entering

the congressional race in Massachusetts' Eleventh District, and was elected to Congress on 5 November 1946. Aged twenty-nine, he took his seat in the House of Representatives, where he served three terms, eventually announcing his intention of seeking a Senate seat, and defeating Henry Cabot Lodge to become US Senator for Massachusetts on 4 November 1952. It was to be the start of a career spent entirely in the political arena, and which was to culminate in Kennedy's election, at forty-four, as the youngest-ever President of the United States, and the first Catholic to be elected. The following year was also a milestone in JFK's private life, when, after a string of love affairs, he married the beautiful socialite, Jacqueline Lee Bouvier. Despite the fact that it produced two children – Caroline, born in 1957, and John Jr, in 1960 – the marriage was not untroubled. JFK soon resumed his philandering ways, and his extramarital affairs, both before and after he became president, were numerous. But in public at least, 'Jack and Jackie' maintained an amicable relationship, establishing a reputation, in the eyes of an enraptured media, as a 'golden couple'.

The next two years, during which JFK was establishing a reputation as a hardworking and well-liked senator, were marred by health problems. While recovering from surgery for his recurrent back trouble, JFK worked on his book *Profiles in Courage* – about notable American senators who had taken unpopular stances on principle – a work which was interpreted as an expression of his political ideals, and for which he won the Pulitzer Prize in 1957. But furthering his literary career was not his only concern during the next five years. After losing the vice-presidential nomination to Estes Kefauver of Tennessee, in August 1957, JFK decided to play for higher stakes. On 2 January 1960, Senator Kennedy announced his candidacy for the United States presidency, and on 13 July he was nominated as presidential candidate, choosing Lyndon B. Johnson as his running-mate. A gruelling four months of campaigning followed, at the end of which, on 8 November 1960, John F. Kennedy was elected President of the United States, narrowly beating Richard M. Nixon by 34,227,096 votes to 34,108,546.

John F. Kennedy was sworn in on 20 January as the first US president born in the twentieth century, and delivered a memorable inaugural address, in which he promised a 'new generation' of leadership. Certainly, his first few months in office were marked by a series of bold political moves – raising and extending the minimum wage, investing in education, and establishing the 'Peace Corps' – which further endeared him to his supporters, while infuriating his opponents. In sharp contrast to these liberal domestic policies was the new president's hardline stance on foreign policy. After announcing a programme to build US military strength abroad, JFK attempted to shore up anti-Communist elements in Cuba – resulting in the 'Bay of Pigs' fiasco of April 1961. Paralleling these covert operations, was the launching of the 'space race', with JFK taking a personal interest in the programme, as a way of promoting American values at home and abroad. Russia's successful launch of the first man in space on 12 April was swiftly followed by the American attempt, and the 'new frontier' was declared open.

The anti-Communist initiatives of the early months of JFK's presidency continued into the following year, when he became involved in a confrontation with the Cuban dictator, Fidel Castro, over the siting of Russian missiles in Cuba – 'America's back yard'. Over the next few weeks the conflict rumbled on, coming to a head in October 1962, with the Cuban Missile Crisis. Only after the world had been brought to the brink of war, did the Russian Premier, Khrushchev, agree to back down, and halt the construction of missile bases in Cuba. As JFK ruefully remarked to his aides of that extraordinarily tense few days, 'This is the week I earn my salary.' At home, he was earning his salary too, with a programme designed to promote economic stability and improved civil liberties. The president's support for African-American rights was put to the test in May 1963, with the outbreak of race riots in Alabama, and JFK made an impassioned plea to the American people in favour of civil rights in his television address on 11 June. Elsewhere in the world, he was promoting his credo of freedom, with powerful speeches such as the one he made at the Berlin Wall on 26 June 1963, in which he declared himself a 'Berliner' and identified with the struggles of 'Iron Curtain' countries against Communist oppression.

Other initiatives dear to JFK's heart included the signing of the nuclear test ban treaty on 26 July 1963 and a tax reduction bill to stimulate the American economy. Sadly, his 'War on Poverty Program for 1964' – announced on 21 November – was never to be put into action. On 22 November 1963, while on his way to give a speech in Dallas, Texas, President Kennedy was assassinated as he was travelling with his wife in an open car, and was pronounced dead at Parkland Memorial Hospital. His supposed assassin, Lee Harvey Oswald, was shot and killed by Jack Ruby on 24 November while in the custody of the Dallas police. On 25 November, John Fitzgerald Kennedy was buried with full military honours at the Arlington National Cemetery in Washington. The House Select Committee on Assassinations, called to reinvestigate the deaths of President Kennedy and civil rights leader Martin Luther King, completed a two-year investigation in 1979 with the conclusion that a conspiracy was 'likely' and that organized crime figures were 'probably' involved. Thus ended – in a mystery which seems to have deepened with the passing years – the life and career of this most brilliant and visionary of political figures.

Handsome, clever and charming, JFK was a 'wit' in every sense of the word: funny, but also sharply intelligent; playful, but also passionately committed. With a gift for repartee and ad-lib honed during the punishing months he spent on the campaign trail, and a fondness for polished quips (for example, 'Washington is a city of Southern efficiency and Northern charm') he displayed a relish for language perhaps only to be expected in one of Irish descent. In one of his last speeches, at the dedication of the Robert Frost Library at Amherst, Massachusetts, he spoke of the importance of poetry in a world increasingly dominated by pragmatism: 'When power leads man toward arrogance, poetry reminds him of his limitations . . . When power corrupts, poetry cleanses.' John F. Kennedy was a man who had a respect for literature and the arts, and who, during his brief time in office, made clear his support for cultural and intellectual innovation. His recorded 'wit' does not consist merely of political point-scoring – although some of his shafts against his opponents are very funny – but displays the whole range of the man. As one of his admirers said, a few years after JFK's death, 'Future generations will surely be quoting our late president.'

CHRISTINA KONING
2003

JFK:
Political Philosopher

John F. Kennedy's presidency lasted a little more than a thousand days, during which time he addressed some of the most important issues of the day: the threat of nuclear war, the emerging civil rights movement, the embryonic women's rights movement and the abolition of poverty and low pay; themes he returned to time and again in his political pronouncements. A man of ready, shrewd and, occasionally, acerbic humour, John F. Kennedy was a liberal by inclination, and was at his most impassioned in defence of a number of principles – freedom of conscience, civil rights, the promotion of global peace – that formed the bedrock of his political credo.

'I'm an idealist without illusions.'

(JFK on his political credo)

✽

'Forgive your enemies, but never forget their names.'

✽

'Things do not happen. They are made to happen.'

✽

'Mothers all want their sons to become President, but they don't want them to become politicians in the process.'

When he was a young congressman, John F. Kennedy was once seen parking his car flagrantly in front of a 'No Parking' sign in downtown Washington.

'This is what Hamlet means,' he explained, 'by "the insolence of office".'

*

When he was a candidate for Congress, Jack Kennedy appeared one night at a rally with dozens of other candidates. The chairman kept Kennedy waiting until late in the evening while he introduced one speaker after another as 'a young fellow, who came up the hard way.'

Finally, sometime after midnight, Jack Kennedy arrived at the podium. He began his speech with the observation, 'I seem to be the only person here tonight who didn't come up the hard way.'

*

President Kennedy's personal secretary, Evelyn Lincoln, recalled first meeting JFK in 1952, when Senator Kennedy was preparing to leave town for Easter recess. He dictated dozens of instructions to another secretary, then added, 'Oh, yes, one last thing. Easter Sunday.' He hesitated as the woman's face sank. 'Yes, Easter Sunday.' He laughed and added, 'You can take Easter Sunday off.'

'You don't fire God.'

(JFK on his reluctance to replace J. Edgar Hoover as Director of the FBI)

*

When one of his White House aides was described by a newspaper as 'coruscatingly brilliant', the President noted, 'Those guys should never forget: 50,000 votes the other way and we'd all be coruscatingly stupid.'

*

'When we [the Democrats] got into office, the thing that surprised me most was to find that things were just as bad as we'd been saying they were.'

(JFK on the Republican administration of his predecessor, President Eisenhower)

*

When a well-meaning friend told Jack Kennedy that he would have no trouble getting the vice-presidential nomination in 1960, he just shook his head.

'Let's not talk so much about vice,' he said. 'I'm against vice in any form.'

'I think "Hail to the Chief" has a nice ring to it.'
(JFK on his favourite tune)

When Bob Hope was honoured in Hollywood on 4 March 1962 for his outstanding work entertaining American servicemen, President Kennedy sent a tape-recorded message. In it he asked Mr Hope to consider making a 'Road to Washington' film: 'From my own experience, I can tell him it's not the easiest road to travel, but it will give him a chance to visit his money – at least what's left of it.'

'There is no city in the United States in which I get a warmer welcome and less votes that Columbus, Ohio.'
(6 January 1962)

'As they say in my own Cape Cod, a rising tide lifts all the boats.'
(Remark made in Frankfurt, Germany, 25 June 1963)

'We're heading into nut country today.'
    (Remark made to his wife in Fort Worth, Texas,
        a few hours before his assassination in Dallas)

'I am delighted that John Bailey's going to take over this job,' commented JFK wryly on the latter's becoming Chairman of the Democratic National Committee. 'He is more popular today than he will be at any time again in his life. I will feel that he is doing a good job when you all say, "Well, Kennedy is all right, but Bailey's the one who is really making the mistakes."'

'There is an old saying that only in the winter can you tell which trees are evergreens.'
    (Remark made to Peace Corps volunteers,
        22 June 1962)

'Do not pray for easy lives,' urged President Kennedy at a prayer breakfast in Washington. 'Pray to be stronger men.'

'My experience in government is that when things are non-controversial, beautifully co-ordinated and all the rest, it must be that there is not much going on.'

'There are not so many differences between politics and football. Some Republicans have been unkind enough to suggest that my close election was somewhat similar to the Notre Dame–Syracuse game [won by Notre Dame with a disputed penalty]. But I am like Notre Dame. We just take it as it comes along. We're not giving it back.

Politics is an astonishing profession. It has enabled me to go from being an obscure member of the junior varsity at Harvard to being an honorary member of the Football Hall of Fame.'

(National Football Foundation dinner,
New York City, December 1961)

'The three most overrated things in the world are the state of Texas, the FBI, and hunting trophies.'

At a Democratic fund-raising dinner in Miami, honouring Senator George A. Smathers of Florida, President Kennedy made these remarks: 'Senator Smathers has been one of my most valuable counsellors at crucial moments. In 1952, when I was thinking of running for the United States Senate, I went to Senator Smathers and said, "George, what do you think?" He said, "Don't do it, can't win, bad year."' (That was the year Mr Kennedy won his Senate seat.) 'In 1956, I didn't know whether I should run for vice president or not so I said, "George, what do you think?" And Senator Smathers replied, "It's your choice!" So I ran and lost. In 1960, I was wondering whether I ought to run in the West Virginia primary, but the senator said, "Don't do it. That state you can't possibly carry." And actually the only time I really got nervous about the whole matter of Los Angeles was just before the balloting and George came up and said, "I think it looks pretty good for you."'

(11 March 1962)

On the Campaign Trail

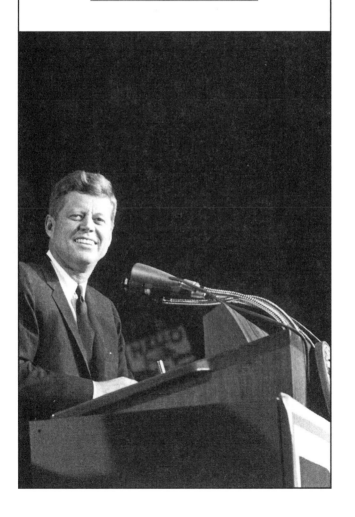

The punishing schedule of campaigning was something JFK endured with his customary wit and vigour. Despite the health problems that plagued him throughout the period leading up to, and after, he was elected president, he managed to project an impression of youth, energy and boundless good humour on the campaign trail, as this selection shows.

In 1958 there were three leading Democratic front runners for the 1960 presidential nomination: John F. Kennedy, Stuart Symington, and Lyndon Baines Johnson.

JFK liked to tell the story of a dream he had about the three of them: 'Several nights ago I dreamed that the good Lord touched me on the shoulder and said, "Don't worry, you'll be the Democratic presidential nominee in 1960. What's more, you'll be elected." I told Stu Symington about the dream. "Funny thing," said Stu, "I had exactly the same dream about myself." We both told our dreams to Lyndon Johnson and he said, "That's funny. For the life of me, I can't remember tapping either of you two boys for the job."'

'I have been, in the last three days, in eight states,' announced JFK on arrival in the Bronx, 5 November 1960. 'Among them California, New Mexico, Arizona, Ohio, Illinois, Virginia, and the Bronx, the ninth state.'

At a campaign stop in 1960, Jack Kennedy tried to elicit a kiss from the shy four-year-old daughter of his friend Paul Fay. Unimpressed by JFK's charm, the little girl resisted, squirming and wriggling in his arms, until he laughed and handed her back to her father, saying, 'I don't think she quite caught the strong quality of love of children, so much a part of the candidate's make-up which has made him so dear to the hearts of all mothers.'

When campaigning for the Senate in the Irish wards of Massachusetts, Jack Kennedy liked to tell the story of the little old Irish widow. 'She came to the ward leader with a complaint that the officials wouldn't accept the answer she gave to a question they asked her about her late husband, which was, "What did he die of?" When the ward leader asked her what the answer was, the little old Irish lady answered, "He died of a Tuesday, I remember it well."'

John Kennedy suffered painful abrasions on his right hand from excessive handshaking during the 1960 presidential campaign, which left his hand bruised, callused and swollen. He raised his sore hand and remarked, 'With all that handshaking, this is probably the greatest right hand in America today!'

Campaigning to win the West Virginia primary, Jack Kennedy visited a mine and mingled with the miners.

'Is it true you're the son of one of our wealthiest men?' asked one of the miners.

JFK admitted it was true.

'Is it true that you've never wanted for anything and have everything you want?'

JFK hesitated. 'I guess so.'

'Is it true you've never done a day's work with your hands all your life?'

JFK nodded.

'Well, let me tell you this,' said the miner. 'You haven't missed a thing.'

Arriving late for breakfast in Wyoming on the campaign trail in 1960, JFK cleared his throat: 'I first of all want to express on behalf of my sister and myself our gratitude to all of you for being kind enough to have this breakfast and make it almost lunch.'

'I know there are some Republicans and some Democrats who say that they have now developed a wonderful arrangement in Washington,' JFK remarked during the 1960 presidential campaign. 'The congress is Democratic and the President is Republican, and nothing happens, and isn't it wonderful?'

'What are we going to do about the Republicans? They can point to Benjamin Harrison, who, according to legend, saw a man forced by the Depression to eat grass on the White House lawn and had only one suggestion for him – that he go around to the back where the grass was longer.'

(Springfield, Illinois, 3 October 1960)

JFK enjoyed neutralizing insults by accepting them as compliments. 'Just before you met,' he told a convention in New York in September 1960, 'a weekly news magazine with a wide circulation featured a section "Kennedy's Liberal Promises" and described me, and I quote, as "the farthest-out Liberal Democrat around", unquote. While I am not certain of the beatnik definition of "farthest-out", I am certain that it was not intended as a compliment.'

John Kennedy accepted a barb from Richard Nixon in the cut-and-thrust of the 1960 campaign: 'Someone was kind enough, though I don't know whether he meant it kindly, to say the other night that in my campaign in California I sounded like Truman with a Harvard accent.'

Asked whether he thought he would lose any votes because of his Catholic religion, John F. Kennedy answered: 'I feel as a Catholic that I'll get my reward in my life hereafter, although I may not get it here.'

'Will Rogers once said that it is not the original investment in a Congressman that counts; it is the upkeep.'

(Alton, Illinois, 3 October 1960)

'Ladies and gentlemen, I was warned to be out here in plenty of time to permit those who are going to the Green Bay Packers game to leave. I don't mind running against Mr Nixon but I have the good sense not to run against the Green Bay Packers.'

(Green Bay, Wisconsin, October 1960)

*

'Senator, when does your moratorium end on Nixon's hospitalization and your ability to attack him?' asked a reporter during the 1960 presidential campaign.

'Well, I said I would not mention him unless I could praise him, until he got out of the hospital,' answered John Kennedy diplomatically, 'and I have not mentioned him.'

Once when Nixon was ahead in the polls, and things looked bad for the Kennedy camp, JFK was heard to say, 'Do you realize the responsibility I carry? I'm the only person standing between Nixon and the White House.'

'Mr Nixon, like the rest of us, has had his troubles in this campaign. At one point even the *Wall Street Journal* was criticizing his tactics. That is like the *Osservatore Romano* criticizing the Pope. One of the inspiring notes that was struck in the last debate was struck by the Vice President in his very moving warning to the candidates against the use of profanity by presidents and ex-presidents when they are on the stump. And I know after fourteen years in the Congress with the Vice President, that he was very sincere in his views about the use of profanity. But I am told that a prominent Republican said to him yesterday in Jacksonville, Florida, "Mr Vice President, that was a damn fine speech." And the Vice President said, "I appreciate the compliment but not the language." And the Republican went on, "Yes sir, I liked it so much that I contributed a thousand dollars to your campaign." And Mr Nixon replied, "The hell you say."'

'However, I would not want to give the impression that I am taking former President Truman's use of language lightly. I have sent him the following wire: "Dear Mr President, I have noted with interest your suggestion as to where those who vote for my opponent should go. While I understand and sympathize with your deep motivation, I think it is important that our side try to refrain from raising the religious issue."'

(Alfred E. Smith Memorial Dinner,
New York City, 19 October 1960)

*

'Mr Nixon, in the last seven days, has called me an economic ignoramus, a Pied Piper, and all the rest. I've just confined myself to calling him a Republican, but he says that is getting low.'

(New York City, 5 November 1960)

*

'Mr Nixon trots out the same old programme. He has given it new names, Operation Consume and Operation Safeguard. But the words are the same, the melody is the same. Only the lighting and make-up are different.'

(La Crosse, Wisconsin,
23 October 1960)

'How can any farmer vote Republican in 1960? I understand nearby there was a farmer who planted some corn. He said to his neighbour, "I hope I break even this year. I really need the money."'

Kennedy's voice rose.

'The farmer is the only man in our economy who buys everything at retail, sells everything at wholesale, and pays the freight both ways.'

Kennedy's voice rose higher.

'What's wrong with the American fah-mah today?'

JFK, with his Cape Cod accent, was passionately addressing a group of farmers in Sioux City, Iowa, about the agricultural depression.

As he paused dramatically for a moment, one of the farmers yelled out, 'He's stah-ving!'

The audience laughed, and so did JFK.

Speaking at a $100-a-plate fund-raising dinner in Salt Lake City, JFK quipped: 'I am deeply touched – not as deeply touched as you have been by coming to this dinner, but nevertheless, it is a sentimental occasion.'

(Salt Lake City, Utah, 23 September 1960)

'I have been informed that with this dinner I am now responsible as the leader of the Democratic Party for a debt of over one million dollars. I don't know – they spend it like they were sure we were going to win.'

'There is a story about a Texan who went to New York and told a New Yorker that he could jump off the Empire State Building and live. The easterner said, "Well, that would be an accident." He said, "Suppose I did it twice?" The easterner said, "That would be an accident, too." "Suppose I did it three times?" And the easterner said, "That would be a habit."

Texas twice, in 1952 and 1956, jumped off the Democratic bandwagon. We are down here to see it is not going to be a habit.'

(El Paso, Texas, 12 September 1960)

'I must say I hope I have normal courage as a politician and candidate for office,' said JFK to a union convention in Portland, Oregon. 'But I don't have quite enough courage to settle the dispute as to whether we should have craft unions or industrial unions. I will let you gentlemen settle that.'

'I'm glad to be here because I feel a sense of kinship with the Pittsburgh Pirates. Like my candidacy, they were not given much chance in the spring.'

(Harrisburg, Pennsylvania, September 1960)

'I don't see how the Flint High School football team ever loses any football game with that cheering section. If they are not busy for the next two months in school, we will be glad to take them with us all around the United States.'

(Flint, Michigan, 5 September 1960)

'I want to express my regrets for being late. They told me five days ago a storm was coming up here, so we waited.'

(Columbia, South Carolina,
10 October 1960)

In a speech on the University of Illinois campus, Mr Kennedy made reference to his famous television debates with Mr Nixon in the following remark: 'A good deal of comparison, and most of it unfavourable, is drawn between the Lincoln-Douglas debates and my weekly brief appearance on *What's Our Line?* every Friday night.'

(24 October 1960)

JFK shrugged off Richard Nixon's supposed 'experience' advantage.

'Mr Nixon may be very experienced in his kitchen debates. So are a great many married men I know.'

At a press conference in Anchorage, Alaska, during the 1960 presidential campaign, Mr Kennedy was asked the following question:

'Senator, you were promised a military intelligence briefing from the President. Have you received that?'

To which Kennedy replied: 'Yes, I talked on Thursday morning to General Wheeler from the Defense Department.'

'What was his first name?' asked the questioner.

'He didn't brief me on that,' quipped Kennedy.

'This week I had the opportunity to debate with Mr Nixon. I feel that I should reveal that I had a great advantage in that debate and I am not referring to anyone's make-up man. The advantage that I had was that Mr Nixon had just debated with Khrushchev, and I had debated with Hubert Humphrey, and that gave me an edge.'

(Minneapolis, Minnesota,
1 October 1960)

John F. Kennedy campaigned hard in Alaska and lost there in 1960. He never visited Hawaii at all and won handily.

A thinker as well as a man of action, JFK remarked, 'Just think what my margin might have been if I had never left home!'

Much was said during the campaign about the relative experience of Mr Kennedy and Mr Nixon. On this point, Mr Kennedy made these remarks in a speech he made in Jacksonville, Florida in October 1960:

'I know a banker who served thirty years as president of a bank. He had more experience, until his bank went broke, than any other banker in Massachusetts. But if I ever go into the banking business, I do not plan to hire him, and he knows the operation from top to bottom.'

On the same issue, Mr Kennedy had this to say to a rally in Minneapolis in October 1960: 'Ladies and gentlemen, the outstanding news story of this week was not the events of the United Nations or even the presidential campaign. It was a story coming out of my own city of Boston that Ted Williams of the Boston Red Sox had retired from baseball. It seems that at forty-two he was too old. It shows that perhaps experience isn't enough.'

'I want to thank that band. One more chorus of "Anchors Aweigh" and we will just float this building right out.'

(Akron, Ohio, September 1960)

'I was informed when I started out this morning that we were going to travel in Delaware County, which voted eight to one for Alf Landon. We are going to wipe that record out. No county in the United States should have that reputation.'

(Norristown, Pennsylvania, October 1960)

'First, we will not rely on a monetary policy that puts its emphasis on tight money and high interest rates. The fact of the matter is, as Frank Church said in his keynote speech, if Rip Van Winkle went to sleep and he woke up and he wanted to know whether the Republicans or the Democrats were in office, he would just say, "How high are the interest rates?"'

(Saginaw, Michigan, 14 October 1960)

'I do not want it said of our generation what T. S. Eliot wrote in his poem, "The Rock" – "and the wind shall say: 'these were decent people, their only monument the asphalt road and a thousand lost golf balls.'" We can do better than that.'

(Columbus, Ohio, 17 October 1960)

Commenting on the punishing schedule he and the other candidates were forced to undergo during the months of campaigning, Kennedy allowed himself a sly dig at the considerably more relaxed timetable of the presidential incumbent: 'This isn't the way they told me it was when I first decided to run for the presidency. After reading about the schedules of the president, I thought we all stayed in bed until ten or eleven, and then got out and drove around.'

(Rockford, Illinois, 24 October 1960)

Prior to the nomination of Lyndon B. Johnson as the Democratic vice-presidential candidate, there were rumours that Governor Pat Brown of California was interested in the nomination. This presented problems for Mr Kennedy, because Governor Brown was also a Catholic – and two Catholics running on the same ticket was not a 'balanced ticket' as far as the electorate was concerned. In a speech in California, Kennedy had this to say: 'I know there has been talk out there about a Kennedy-Brown ticket, and I sincerely wish that we could arrange that. Unfortunately, I come from Massachusetts and the governor comes from California, and I don't believe the country is ready for a ticket that stretches from the Atlantic to the Pacific.'

On the campaign trail, presidential candidates had to be prepared to make a speech at any hour of the day – sometimes after a lengthy and exhausting journey. Commenting on this problem, Kennedy remarked, in a speech in Anchorage, Alaska in September 1960: 'I want to express my appreciation for that warm Alaskan welcome. As Bob Bartlett said, we started out about nine o'clock in the morning from Baltimore and it is now four o'clock in the morning for those of us living on Eastern time. I have not made a speech that late in the evening since some of the early Massachusetts political banquets, which I attended when I was first a congressman, when they would put the junior members on about this hour.'

'I appreciate your welcome. As the cow said to the Maine farmer, "Thank you for a warm hand on a cold morning."'

(Los Angeles, California, 2 November 1960)

'I want to express my great appreciation to all of you for your kindness in coming out and giving us a warm Hoosier welcome. I understand that this town suffered a misfortune this morning when the bank was robbed. I am confident that the *Indianapolis Star* will say "Democrats Arrive and Bank Robbed". But we don't believe that.'

(Anderson, Indiana, 5 October 1960)

'Ladies and gentlemen, the devices which are used in the City of New York to separate you from your life savings are numerous. When the dinners run out, the luncheons begin, and when the luncheons run out, the breakfasts begin. We may all meet next week to get the campaign out of the red with a midnight brunch at eighty-five dollars a person – and I will be there.'

(New York City, 5 November 1960)

'I come to Suffolk County and ask your help. If we can do well in this county, and I ask your help in doing well, we're going to put this speech to music and make a fortune out of it.'

(Commack, Long Island, New York, 6 November 1960)

'Ladies and gentlemen, it is my understanding that the last candidate for the presidency to visit this community in a presidential year was Herbert Hoover in 1928. President Hoover initiated on the occasion of his visit the slogan "Two chickens for every pot", and it is no accident that no presidential candidate has ever dared come back to this community.'

(Bristol, Tennessee, 21 September 1960)

During the campaign, Kennedy often remarked about the long and tough role of campaigning. He made these remarks on that subject in a speech in Dayton, Ohio:

'Franklin Roosevelt started his campaign here in Ohio. I don't know what has happened to politics, but whenever I read about the 1932 campaign, Franklin Roosevelt stayed in Albany all winter, spring, summer, didn't go to the convention until he was nominated. He then took a boating trip up the coast of Maine with his son, started his campaign late in September, made some speeches, and was elected by a tremendous majority.'

(17 October 1960)

After receiving a very flattering introduction from a fellow Democrat during the 1960 presidential campaign in Michigan, Jack Kennedy responded with graceful wit:

'I want to express my appreciation to the Governor. Every time he introduces me as the potentially greatest president in the history of the United States, I always think perhaps he is overstating it by one or two degrees. George Washington wasn't a bad president and I do want to say a word for Thomas Jefferson. But, otherwise, I will accept the compliment.'

(Muskegon, Michigan, 5 September 1960)

'I personally have lived through ten presidential campaigns, but I must say the eleventh makes me feel like I lived through twenty-five.'

(New York City, 14 September 1960)

QUESTION: 'Senator, Governor Pat Brown today issued a very optimistic statement. Yet a poll shows Nixon running ahead. Which of these two experts do you believe?'

MR KENNEDY: 'I believe Governor Brown.'

(Burbank, California,
9 September 1960)

'I come from a non-agricultural state, Massachusetts, and therefore, I am sure that there are some farmers in Iowa and South Dakota who say, "Why should we elect someone from New England? Why shouldn't we elect a farmer?" Well, there is no farmer up for the office this year. Whittier, California is not one of the great agricultural sections of the United States.'

(Sioux City, Iowa, 21 September 1960)

'Ladies and gentlemen, I want to express my appreciation to all of you being kind enough to wait at the airport for my sister and myself, and also my regrets at being so late. In case any of you wanted to run for the presidency, I would say we started this morning in Iowa, we spoke in South Dakota, we speak now in North Dakota, we speak at a dinner meeting in Montana, and end up in Wyoming tonight. I think that my election chief thinks that the election is October 8 rather than November 8.'

(Fargo, North Dakota,
22 September 1960)

'I want to express my thanks to all of you, particularly those of you who are college students and can't vote, who came down here anyway. I recognize that the sacrifice is not extensive as I am doing all the work this morning and you are not in class. I am glad that you are participating happily in the political process. Artemus Ward, fifty years ago, said, "I am not a politician and my other habits are also good."'

(Albion, Michigan, 14 October 1960)

'Texas has sent twenty-one Democratic Congressmen to Congress and one Republican, a fair proportion, a good average.'

(El Paso, Texas, 12 September 1960)

[45]

'Last week a noted clergyman was quoted as saying that our society may survive in the event of my election, but it certainly won't be what it was. I would like to think he was complimenting me, but I'm not sure he was.'

(New York City, 14 September 1960)

'We don't want to be like the leader in the French Revolution who said, "There go my people. I must find out where they are going so I can lead them."'

'We know they will invoke the name of Abraham Lincoln on behalf of their candidate – despite the fact that the political career of their candidate has often seemed to show charity toward none and malice for all.'

(JFK on his Republican opponents [Abraham Lincoln's second inaugural address, 4 March 1865, includes the line, 'With malice toward none; with charity for all . . .'])

'I regret the rain, but it rains, as the Bible tells us, on the just and the unjust alike, on Republicans as well as Democrats.'

(Sioux Falls, South Dakota, 22 September 1960)

'Those of you who live in this State of Florida depend upon a moving and expanding country. I know something about the economy of this state. When the rest of the country catches cold, Florida gets pneumonia and Miami is very sick.'

(Miami, Florida, 18 October 1960)

✳

During the 1960 campaign a reporter in Los Angeles asked facetiously: 'Do you think a Protestant can be elected president in 1960?'

JFK answered: 'If he's prepared to answer how he stands on the issue of separation of church and state, I see no reason why we should discriminate against him.'

✳

'This state knows the issues of this campaign – senior citizens. Senator McNamara is chairman of the Senate Committee on Senior Citizens. I am vice chairman. We are both ageing fast.'

(Warren, Michigan, 26 October 1960)

✳

On election night in 1960 Jack Kennedy received a long-distance call from his running-mate, Lyndon B. Johnson. Grinning, JFK reported to his staff what LBJ had said to him: 'I hear *you're* losing in Ohio, but *we're* doing fine in Pennsylvania.'

'You remember the very old story about a citizen of Boston who heard a Texan talking about the glories of Bowie, Davy Crockett and the rest, and finally said, "Haven't you heard of Paul Revere?" To which the Texan answered, "Well, he is the man who ran for help."'

(Houston, Texas, 12 September 1960)

When a public address system failed during a campaign stop in St Paul, Minnesota, JFK remarked: 'I understand that Daniel Webster used to address a hundred thousand people without any trouble at all, and without a mike, so it should be easy for us. However, we are a little softer than they used to be.'

'The man in the audience said that I should tell Mr Nixon that experience is what he will have left after this campaign is over. I don't know why we never think of these things.'

Witty Words
from the
White House

President Kennedy moved with his wife Jackie and their young family – three-year-old daughter Caroline and infant son, John Jr – into the White House in 1961, following the President's inauguration on 20 January. The presence of such young children in the historical residence made it a real family home for the first time in its history. During the years of JFK's incumbency, artists, writers, musicians and scientists were amongst those invited to enjoy the presidential hospitality, and this intellectual vibrancy, combined with the elegant modernization of the interior, which was carried out under the eye of the First Lady, established the Kennedy White House as a centre for social and cultural life.

On his first day in the White House, President Kennedy noticed that his personal secretary, Evelyn Lincoln, had his reading copy of his inaugural address on her desk.

'I read the other day that one of the former presidents was offered $75,000 for his inaugural address,' he said. 'Mrs Lincoln, give me a pen so I can sign mine.'

JFK signed his inaugural address and said, 'Here, Mrs Lincoln, keep this $75,000 for me!'

'Washington is a city of Southern efficiency and Northern charm.'

(quoted by William Manchester
in *Portrait of a President*)

At a Washington dinner party shortly after his inauguration, President Kennedy paid tribute to Washington lawyer Clark Clifford, who had served as Mr Kennedy's representative to the Eisenhower administration during the period of transition immediately after Mr Kennedy's election: 'Clark is a wonderful fellow. In a day when so many are seeking a reward for what they contributed to the return of the Democrats to the White House, you don't hear Clark clamouring. He was invaluable to us and all he asked in return was that we advertise his law firm on the backs of one-dollar bills.'

(February 1961)

'The pay is good and I can walk to work.'
(JFK on being President)

In tribute to Senator Warren Magnuson of Washington, President Kennedy described Magnuson's Senate technique: 'He never visits the Senate until late in the afternoon when almost everybody has gone home. He comes in at the last minute and waits until he can have the floor, and then he says, "What's my business? Oh, it's nothing important. Just the Grand Coulee Dam!"'

At a birthday dinner for Ohio Governor DiSalle in Columbus, Ohio, on 6 January 1962, President Kennedy began his remarks with a historical footnote:

'A hundred years ago, Abraham Lincoln stayed up all night in a telegraph office, watching the results of an essential gubernatorial contest in this state, in the darkest days of the Civil War. And at the end of the night when the Unionist candidate who supported Lincoln's policies had finally emerged as the winner, Lincoln wired, "Glory to God in the highest, Ohio has saved the nation."

Two years ago yesterday, when Governor DiSalle was kind enough to endorse my candidacy, I had somewhat similar sentiments about Ohio.'

'It would be premature to ask for your support in the next election and it would be inaccurate to thank you for it in the past.'
(Address to National Industrial Conference Board, Washington, DC, 13 February 1961)

When a reporter told the President that a reputable columnist said the attitude of big business was, 'Now we have you where we want you,' JFK shook his head and said, 'I can't believe I'm where big business wants me.'

'Many businessmen who are prospering as never before during this administration are convinced, nevertheless, that we must be anti-business,' President Kennedy told the Tampa Chamber of Commerce. 'When our bill to grant a tax credit for business investment was before the Congress, Secretary of the Treasury Dillon was on a plane to this state, and he found himself talking to one of the leading Florida businessmen about the investment tax credit. He spent some time, he later told me, explaining how the bill would help this man's corporate outlook and income, and the businessman was most impressed. Finally, as the plane landed at Miami, he turned to Secretary Dillon and said, "I am very grateful to you for explaining the bill. Now tell me just once more why it is that I am against it?"'

'My father always told me that all businessmen were sons of bitches, but I never believed it till now.'

'A dilemma, it seems to me, is posed by the occasion of a presidential address to a business group less than four weeks after entering the White House,' the President said, while addressing a National Industrial Conference in February 1961, 'for it is too early to be claiming credit for the new administration and too late to be blaming the old one.'

'I don't know whether you realize that this is an historic occasion. We have paid off nearly $4,000,000 that the Kennedy–Johnson ticket ran up in November of 1960. It is now gone forever, which is sad, and all we have left is the Federal deficit.'

✳

Barry Goldwater, a senator from Arizona and a champion of conservatism (whose 1964 presidential candidacy would later launch a revolution within the Republican Party), was an excellent photographer. He once took a good picture of President Kennedy and sent it to him for an autograph. The picture came back with the inscription: 'For Barry Goldwater, whom I urge to follow the career for which he has shown so much talent – photography. From his friend, John Kennedy.'

✳

Soon after President Kennedy blocked the steel price hike in 1961, as he enjoyed recounting, he was visited by a prominent businessman who was gloomy about the economy.

'Things look great,' JFK reassured the businessman. 'Why, if I weren't President, I'd be buying stock myself.'

'If you weren't President,' replied the businessman, 'so would I.'

Strolling through the replanted White House gardens, President Kennedy gazed admiringly at the flowerbeds, saying, 'This may go down as the real achievement of this administration.'

JFK was vitally interested in the renovation of the White House and its grounds. When the Rose Garden was being torn up and replanted, he would periodically call out of the White House window to the men digging the garden, 'Struck oil yet?'

President Kennedy was proud of the sophisticated telephone operating system in the White House, and boasted that its operators could find anyone, anywhere, at any hour of the day or night. Once JFK dared Jackie and some friends to come up with the name of someone the operators couldn't find.

Jackie suggested Truman Capote because he had an unlisted number.

JFK picked up the telephone and said only, 'Yes, this is the President. Would you please get me Truman Capote?' No further identification was given or requested.

Thirty minutes later Truman Capote was on the line. He was not located at his own number in Brooklyn, but at the home of a friend in Palm Springs, another unlisted number.

Informed that the millionth tourist during his term of office was about to walk through the White House, President Kennedy asked, 'Will he be a Cuban or a freedom fighter or a woman in shorts?'

✳

The Kennedy White House was known for its style. Jack Kennedy could appreciate style, grace and eloquence anywhere, anytime.

French President Charles de Gaulle sent President Kennedy a letter urging him not to negotiate. The President read the letter excitedly to several colleagues, praising its style: 'Isn't that beautiful?'

'You agree with it?' asked one of his astonished listeners, knowing the President had ideas that sharply opposed those of De Gaulle.

'Oh no!' exclaimed JFK. 'But what a marvellous style!'

✳

'I suppose a number of things attract us all here today. Some of us will think it wise to associate as much as possible with historians and cultivate their good will, though we always have the remedy which Winston Churchill once suggested when he prophesied during World War II that history would deal gently with us. "Because," Mr Churchill said, "I intend to write it!"'

(Washington, DC, 3 October 1961)

An international incident was barely averted when Canadian Prime Minister Diefenbacker angrily charged that President Kennedy had written 'S.O.B.' on some official State Department document concerning the Canadian Prime Minister and Canada.

The Canadian Prime Minister refused to release the controversial document, even after JFK denied having written the offending words.

JFK shrugged it off, saying he wondered why the Canadian Prime Minister didn't do 'what any normal government would do . . . make a photostatic copy, and return the original.'

Leonard Lyons informed President Kennedy of the going rate for signed portrait photos of presidents, past and present: Franklin D. Roosevelt – $75; U. S. Grant – $55; John F. Kennedy – $65.

JFK wrote back:

Dear Leonard

I appreciate your letter about the market on Kennedy signatures. It is hard to believe that the going price is so high now. In order not to depress the market further, I will not sign this letter.

Urging passage of his education bill, President Kennedy in his second State of the Union address on 11 January 1962, quoted H. G. Wells. '"Civilization," said H. G. Wells, "is a race between education and catastrophe." It is up to you in this Congress to determine the winner of that race.'

Under fire from critics of his economic policies, President Kennedy turned to his economic adviser, Walter Heller, and said, 'Walter, I want to make it perfectly clear that I resent these attacks on you.'

The 'religious issue' was Kennedy's Catholicism in a country which had never elected a Catholic president. Hearing that he was criticized by the Vatican for his statements that he would not be influenced by the Vatican, Senator Kennedy smiled sadly and said, 'Now I understand why Henry VIII set up his own church.'

'Speaking of the religious issue,' JFK joked to White House correspondents, 'I asked the Chief Justice whether he thought our new education bill was constitutional and he said, "It's clearly constitutional – it hasn't got a prayer."'

'Once again, Berlin and the Federal Republic have spoiled us for home,' JFK acknowledged an enthusiastic reception in Berlin on 26 June 1963. 'Now, when we don't get a million people out for a political speech in Worcester, Massachusetts or Danbury, Connecticut, everyone, especially the reporters, is going to write that there are signs of apathy in the United States. And when we have a crowded dinner of fifty at the White House, I am afraid this dinner is going to throw a pall on the entire affair.'

President Kennedy played host to President Ayub Khan of Pakistan at Mount Vernon. Secretary of the Interior Udall was chatting with President Ayub's daughter and told her he had climbed a certain mountain in Pakistan. Unfortunately, Secretary Udall was mistaken; the mountain to which he was referring was in neighbouring Afghanistan and was hotly disputed. President Kennedy happened to overhear the Secretary's mistake and came to the rescue by saying: 'Madam, that is why I named Mr Udall Secretary of the *Interior*.'

President Kennedy made the most of an Ivory Coast toast. 'I do not think that any visitor to our country has had a more constructive career than our distinguished guest of honour,' said the American President, toasting President Houphouet-Boigny of the Ivory Coast. 'And I am not alone referring to the fact that in a free election he was elected by 98 per cent of the voters of his country – a record which has not been equalled recently in the United States – and from what I read, will not be.'

When Indian Prime Minister Jawaharlal Nehru visited the White House, President Kennedy was uncomfortable with the latter's tendency to remain silent. Later it was remarked that Nehru seemed to be interested and vivacious only when conversing with the First Lady. The President nodded knowingly and smiled: 'A lot of our visiting statesmen have the same trouble.'

President Kennedy took Prime Minister Nehru on a boat trip aboard his boat, the *Honey Fitz*, sailing past the plush mansions of Newport, Rhode Island.

The President turned to Nehru and said, 'I wanted you to see how the average American family lives.'

On a return visit to the White House, former President Truman entertained President Kennedy and the assembled dinner guests with a few selections on the piano. President Kennedy was quoted as having made this comment, after Mr Truman had finished his recital: 'Don't say there is no justice in the world. Stalin has been kicked out of Lenin's tomb and President Truman is back in the White House.'

(5 November 1961)

'I want to say that I have been in on-the-job training for about eleven months and feel that I have some seniority rights.

I am delighted to be here with you and with the Secretary of Labor, Arthur Goldberg. I was up in New York, stressing physical fitness, and in line with that, Arthur went over with a group to Switzerland to climb some of the mountains there. They got up about five and he was in bed. He got up to join them later and when they all came back at four o'clock in the afternoon he didn't come back with them.

So they sent out search parties and there was not a sign that afternoon and night. The next day the Red Cross went out and around calling, "Goldberg, Goldberg! It's the Red Cross!" Then this voice came down from the mountain: "I gave at the office."

Those are the liberties you can take with members of the cabinet.'

(AFL-CIO Convention, Bal Harbour, Florida, 7 December 1961)

Jack Kennedy liked to play the humorous nickname game with close friends. JFK's nickname for Lyndon Baines Johnson was 'Landslide'. It was a teasing reference to the fact that LBJ was first elected to the Senate in the primary by a scant margin of eighty-seven votes. President Kennedy addressed his Vice President as 'Lyndon' however. LBJ was so sensitive that JFK said writing a birthday telegram to him was 'like drafting a state document'.

In April 1961 President Kennedy decided to send Vice President Johnson to visit a number of Asian countries, including Vietnam. Johnson was not enthusiastic about going to Saigon and said so.

'Don't worry, Lyndon,' JFK reassured him. 'If anything happens to you, Sam Rayburn [Speaker of the House and a Texan] and I will give you the biggest funeral Austin, Texas, ever saw.'

Ironically, it was John Kennedy whose funeral was next, and it was the biggest the world had ever seen.

The margin of victory for the Kennedy–Johnson ticket in 1960 was slim, but in 1964 Lyndon Johnson won the presidential election by a landslide, fulfilling John Kennedy's ironic nickname.

'Let's see,' President Kennedy liked to say of the latest problems. 'Did we inherit these, or are they our own?'

'I have a few opening announcements,' the President addressed a White House correspondents' dinner in 1962, shortly after his dramatic clash with the steel industry over the increase in steel prices. Demonstrating a talent for self-parody, JFK railed against the rise in dinner ticket prices.

'First, the sudden and arbitrary action of the officers of this organization in increasing the price of dinner tickets by two dollars and fifty cents over the last year constitutes a wholly unjustifiable defiance of the public interest. If this increase is not rescinded but is imitated by the Gridiron, Radio-TV and other dinners, it will have a serious impact on the economy of this city. In this serious hour in our nation's history, when newsmen are awakened in the middle of the night to be given a front-page story, when expense accounts are being scrutinized by the Congress, when correspondents are required to leave their families for long and lonely weekends at Palm Beach, the American people will find it hard to accept this ruthless decision made by a tiny handful of executives whose only interest is in the pursuit of pleasure. I am hopeful that the Women's Press Club will not join this price rise and will thereby force a rescission."

The following note was sent by President Kennedy to Prime Minister Diefenbaker of Canada, after Mr Diefenbaker had expressed his regrets over the fact that President Kennedy had sprained his back in a tree-planting ceremony on the President's recent visit to Canada: 'Many thanks for your gracious message. The tree will be there long after the discomfort is gone.'

(9 June 1961)

Prior to his becoming president, John F. Kennedy was a member of the Harvard Board of Overseers. President Kennedy attended his last meeting as a member of the Board immediately after his election. As he entered the University Hall to attend the last meeting, he was met by cheering students. The new president turned to the students and said: 'I am here to go over your grades with Dr Pusey and I'll protect your interests.'

(9 January 1961)

'I think this is the most extraordinary collection of talent, of human knowledge, that has ever been gathered together at the White House – with the possible exception of when Thomas Jefferson dined alone.'
(White House Dinner honouring
Nobel Prize winners)

In a note to Arthur Hays Sulzberger, chairman of the boards of *The New York Times*, Mr Kennedy had this to say concerning Mr Sulzberger's recent acquisition of a new rocking chair: 'You will recall what Senator Dirksen said about the rocking chair – it gives you a sense of motion without any sense of danger.'

(1 May 1961)

'I recognize tonight that I bear a heavy responsibility of having kept a distinguished group of Americans who paid $125 for this dinner from that dinner for an hour and thirty minutes.

But, I will say that – if I may quote an old East Side expression – what you have lost on bananas, you are going to make up on apples, because this could have been one of the longest dinners in the history of these occasions.

Lyndon [Johnson] is good for forty-five minutes, when he is given a chance; Ambassador Stevenson has been known to go for a very long time; Frank Pace has a very long story to tell; and Bob Hope, will, if called upon. So this might have to go on to one or two in the morning but, because of my imminent journey to Paris, you'll be out – hungry, rather unhappy – but you will be home early tonight.

It is now one-thirty in Paris and I am due there at ten-thirty, and I do not believe it would be a good start to keep the General waiting. So I shall be brief . . .'

(Eleanor Roosevelt Cancer Foundation Dinner, New York City, 30 May 1961)

'Those of you who regard my profession of political life with some disdain should remember that it made it possible for me to move from being an obscure lieutenant in the United States Navy to Commander-in-Chief in fourteen years with very little technical competence.'

(University of North Carolina, 12 October 1961)

❋

In a campaign speech for Richard J. Hughes in his race for the New Jersey Governorship against former Secretary of Labor James P. Mitchell, President Kennedy had this to say:

'One year ago at this time I came to this city around dark having made about fifteen speeches. In the last nine months, I'm happy to say this is the first stump speech I've made for a candidate and I'm glad it's here in New Jersey.

I am somewhat out of practice. But I will say that the last time I came to New Jersey it was just after Mr Nixon had turned down the fifth debate. And I gather that Mr Mitchell feels that no Republican should ever be caught in debate again.'

(2 November 1961)

'For all I have been reading in the last three, four or five months about the great conservative revival sweeping the United States, I thought perhaps no one was going to show up today.'

(Young Democrats Convention, Miami Beach, Florida, December 1961)

During a visit to Paris in June 1961, President Kennedy addressed his hosts in the following speech: 'A few years ago it was said that the optimists learned Russian and the pessimists learned Chinese. I prefer to think that those with vision study French and English.'

Theodore C. Sorenson was a key Kennedy aide and chief speechwriter for the President. Rarely did Mr Sorenson make any speeches of his own. However, he did make one speech in Nebraska in which he criticized their educational system. This speech had many Nebraskans up in arms. When asked about the predicament that Mr Sorenson found himself in, Mr Kennedy remarked: 'That's what happens when you let a speechwriter out on his own.'

(July 1961)

During a ceremony for signing a housing bill, President Kennedy enlivened the occasion with a touch of Shakespeare. Noting the absence of two Alabama Democrats, Representative Albert Rains and Senator John J. Sparkman, who had manoeuvred the bill through Congress, the President declared: 'Having this bill signed without them here is somewhat like having *Hamlet* played without the Prince.'

(Washington, DC, 2 July 1961)

✳

'Football is far too much a sport for the few who can play it well. The rest of us – and too many of our children – get our exercise from climbing up to the seats in stadiums, or from walking across the room to turn on our television sets. And this is true for one sport after another, all across the board.'

(National Football Foundation Hall of Fame banquet, 5 December 1961)

✳

'It has recently been suggested that whether I serve one or two terms in the presidency, I will find myself at the end of that period at what might be called the awkward age, too old to begin a new career and to young to write my memoirs.'

(National Industrial Conference Board, Washington, DC, 13 February 1961)

'This is a double birthday party today. The Children's Bureau is fifty years old and so is Secretary Ribicoff. This is an awkward birthday for the Secretary because he is too young to retire and too old to be President.'

(Fiftieth Anniversary of the United States Children's Bureau, Washington, DC, 8 April 1962)

'I feel at home here because I number in my own state of Massachusetts many friends and former constituents who are of Canadian descent. Their vote is enough to determine the outcome of an election, even a presidential election. You can understand that having been elected President of the United States by less than one hundred and forty thousand votes out of sixty million, that I am very conscious of these statistics.'

'Some years ago, in the city of Fall River, Massachusetts, the Mayor was elected by one vote, and every time he went down the street, everyone would come up to him and say, "Say, Dan, I put you in office."

And I feel a little like that in Chicago tonight. If all of you had voted the other way – there's about fifty-five hundred of you here tonight – I wouldn't be President of the United States.'

Whenever he addressed a meeting of the National Association of Manufacturers, President Kennedy was cognizant of the fact that he was not speaking before the friendliest of audiences. Mr Kennedy opened an address to the NAM in December 1961 with these remarks: 'I understand that President McKinley and I are the only two Presidents of the United States ever to address such an occasion. I suppose that President McKinley and I are the only two that are regarded as fiscally sound enough to be qualified for admission to this organization on an occasion such as this.'

Special ceremonies were held at the White House in November 1961 in honour of the 46th biennial general assembly of the Union of American Hebrew Congregations. At these ceremonies President Kennedy received a gift of a sacred Torah. In accepting the Torah, the President turned to the then Secretary of Labor, Arthur Goldberg, who was a trustee of the Union of American Hebrew Congregations, and said: 'I'll ask the Secretary of Labor to translate this for me.'

'Those of us who had difficulty navigating at sea are astonished at the ability to navigate under ice.'
(White House ceremony honouring submarine and Arctic research scientist Waldo K. Lyon, 7 August 1962)

*

'Last year, more Americans went to symphonies than went to baseball games. This may be viewed as an alarming statistic, but I think that both baseball and the country will endure.'
(White House Youth Concert, 6 August 1962)

*

'It's a vital business, the running of a democracy, and it's important that all of us register and vote for the party of our choice.

I am supporting the party of my choice and I intend to vote in the November elections.'
(Washington, DC, 28 August 1962)

*

After a holiday in Palm Beach, the President returned to Washington, chastened. 'Like members of Congress, I have been, during the last few days over the Easter holiday, back in touch with my constituents and seeing how they felt,' he said, 'and frankly, I have come back to Washington from Palm Beach and I'm against my entire programme.'

In September 1963, at the Salt Lake City airport, Utah, President Kennedy pulled the switch to activate generators at the Green River in the Colorado River basin 150 miles away: 'I never know when I press these whether I am going to blow up Massachusetts or start the project.'

Observing a small boy crawling restlessly back and forth, President Kennedy nodded approval. 'Well, I suppose if you could have only one thing it would be that – energy. Without it, you haven't got a thing.'

Then the President listened intently to the loud-speaker for the voice that was supposed to announce the successful starting of the generators, remarking, 'If we don't hear from him, it's back to the drawing boards.'

'Last week, after speaking to the Chamber of Commerce and the AMA, I began to wonder how I got elected and now I remember . . .

I flew longer – and this will go down in the history books – I flew longer in a helicopter than any President of the United States to come here today. That's the kind of forward-looking administration we have.'

(United Auto Workers Convention,
Atlantic City, New Jersey,
8 May 1962)

'While most segments of the economy are producing more with fewer men than before, Chicago is an exception to the pattern, since it now takes ten men to manage a Chicago Cubs instead of one.'

(Dedication of O'Hare International Airport, Chicago, Illinois, 24 March 1963)

'I'm very proud to be here tonight. I'm particularly interested in the fact that two of our distinguished guests are former Prime Ministers of Peru and are now publishers of newspapers.

It does suggest to those who hold office that when the time comes that if, as they say in the United States, if you can't beat them, join them.'

(Inter-American Press Association, Miami Beach, Florida, 18 November 1963)

'I used to wonder when I was in the House how President Truman got into so much trouble. Now I'm beginning to get the idea . . .'

'Waterbury is either the easiest city to get crowds or it has the best Democrats in the United States.'

(Waterbury, Connecticut, 11 October 1962)

'I'm sorry to see Matt go. He's the only businessman we have left.'
(Washington dinner honouring Matthew McClosky,
former Democratic National Treasurer,
Mayflower Hotel, 10 June 1962)

'I want to register an official protest with the International Ladies' Garment Workers of the sweat-shop conditions under which we are working today. I'm not sure that this represents fifty years of progress. It is true that your distinguished president [David Dubinsky] invited me to come to speak on November 3rd as we were heading to a meeting which he was sponsoring three days before election. I would have agreed to anything.'
(I.L.G.W.U. Housing Project,
New York City, 19 May 1962)

'One Las Vegas gambler is supposed to have said he hoped we'd be as tough on Berlin as we've been on Las Vegas. Well, we intend to be.'
(US Attorneys Meeting,
White House, 10 October 1962)

At a press conference in February of 1961, a reporter asked Mr Kennedy what steps the Government was considering to stop Cuban exports to the USA. He specifically mentioned the shipment of molasses. After discussing the general problem, the President turned to the subject of molasses. He paused for a moment and said: 'I believe it's going to be made into gin – and I'm not sure that's in the public interest.'

President Kennedy was asked to comment on the election of Mayor Robert F. Wagner of New York and Governor Hughes of New Jersey. The reporters wanted to know if the President felt that, since both Mayor Wagner and Governor Hughes were Democrats, that their election indicated that things looked good for the Democrats in future elections.

'They won because they were effective candidates. But they ran as Democrats,' said Kennedy. 'And I believe that it indicates that the American people believe that the candidates and parties in those areas, as well as nationally, are committed to progress. So I am happy, and I suppose some day we will lose and I'll have to eat those words.'

(November 1961)

'Today we celebrate the 110th anniversary of the admission of the State of California into the union. It seems to me that the great story of California has come about because people were not satisfied with things as they were. They liked Massachusetts and they liked Ohio and they liked Oklahoma, but they thought they could do better when it came to California. I don't know why they felt like that about Massachusetts.'

(Modesto, California, 9 September 1960)

John Kennedy always seemed to attract large numbers of very young people to hear his speeches. At Girard, Ohio, he commented on an especially young crowd:

'If we can lower the voting age to nine, we are going to sweep the state.'

'At four o'clock tomorrow, we're going to have a rally here on Medical Care for the Aged. Those who would prefer to stay and wait will find us all back here at the same stand. And in the meantime, let me tell you what a pleasure it is once in a while to get out of Washington and not read the papers, but come and see the voters.'

(New York's Birthday Salute to President Kennedy, Madison Square Gardens, New York City, 19 May 1962)

An eight-year-old girl, Michelle Rochon of Marine City, Michigan, was upset that nuclear tests were being conducted close to the North Pole. Her letter to the President expressing her concerns received this reply from the Chief Executive:

Dear Michelle

I was glad to get your letter about trying to stop the Russians from bombing the North Pole and risking the life of Santa Claus.

I share your concern about the atmospheric testing by the Soviet Union, not only for the North Pole, but for countries throughout the world.

However you must not worry about Santa Claus. I talked with him yesterday and he is fine. He will be making his rounds this Christmas.

[Signed] John F. Kennedy

President Kennedy was criticized by Catholic Church officials for opposing federal aid to parochial schools. After proposing his eduation bill to Congress, JFK quipped, 'As all of you know, some circles invented the myth that after Al Smith's defeat in 1928, he sent a one-word telegram to the Pope: "Unpack." After my press conference on the school bill, I received a one-word wire from the Pope: "Pack."'

'This country reserves its highest honours for only one kind of aristocracy – that which the Founding Fathers called "an aristocracy of achievement arising out of a democracy of opportunity".'

(Message to Congress, 6 June 1963)

President Kennedy could not resist the temptation to tease the Postmaster General. Unable to attend a testimonial luncheon in honour of Postmaster General J. Edward Day, the President sent his regrets and added: 'I am sending this message by wire, since I want to be certain that this message reaches you in the right place at the right time.'

Later a reporter asked: 'Mr President, have you narrowed your search for a new Postmaster General? And are you seeking a man with a business background or a political background?'

JFK replied, 'The search is narrowing, but we haven't – there are other fields that are still being considered, including even a postal background.'

Asked how he liked being President of the United States, JFK shrugged and said simply, 'I have a nice home, the office is close by and the pay is good.'

'The only other president to have visited Ashland was Calvin Coolidge, who never said a word. I was here for only one night and spoke all the time.'

(Ashland, Wisconsin, 24 September 1963)

∗

'The other day I read in a newspaper where Senator Goldwater asked for labour's support before 2,000 cheering Illinois businessmen . . .

Three years ago and one week, by a landslide, the people of the United States elected me to the presidency of this country.'

(AFL-CIO Convention, New York City,
15 November 1963)

∗

At the end of his first year in office, President Kennedy commented: 'The job is interesting, but the possibilities for trouble are unlimited. It's been a tough year, but then, they're all going to be tough.'

Later he was asked, 'If you had to do it all over again would you work for the presidency and would you recommend the job to others?'

'Well, the answer to the first is yes and the answer to the second is no. I don't recommend it to others, at least not for a while.'

After losing the presidential nomination to Estes Kefauver in 1956, Jack Kennedy went on a vacation at his father's rented Riviera home. Michael Canfield, the former husband of Jackie's sister, asked Jack why he wanted to be the American President.

Basking in the sun, his eyes still closed, JFK said, 'I guess it's the only thing I can do.'

That turned out to be true – for him. In Georgetown just before his inauguration, the President-elect said: 'It's a big job. It isn't going to be so bad. You've got time to think. You don't have all those people bothering you that you had in the Senate – besides, the pay is pretty good.'

Despite this and other similar quips, JFK clearly wasn't in it for the money. He donated his presidential salary to charity.

Nearest and Dearest: On JFK's Family and Friends

The close-knit 'Kennedy clan', presided over by matriarch
Rose Kennedy, and by the formidable Joseph Kennedy,
has become something of an American legend – not least
because of the achievement of its most famous son. No less
celebrated – and enigmatic – is the relationship between
JFK and his beautiful wife Jacqueline, who was to
become such an asset to him both in the lead-up to his
election as president and afterwards.

When President Kennedy and the First Lady visited Paris in 1961, Jacqueline, speaking fluent French, charmed everyone, including President de Gaulle. At a press conference shortly before departing for the United States, JFK said farewell to his French hosts: 'I do not think it entirely inappropriate to introduce myself to this audience. I am the man who accompanied Jacqueline Kennedy to Paris, and I have enjoyed it.'

(SHAPE Headquarters,
Paris, 2 June 1961)

✳

During their 1961 visit to France, President Kennedy and Mrs Kennedy stayed in a Quai d'Orsay suite with a gold bathtub. Noting the extravagance, JFK remarked, 'It may seem funny to us, but maybe it's a better use for gold than locking it up in Fort Knox.'

Soon after his inauguration, President Kennedy greeted Madame Herve Alphand, wife of the French ambassador, at a White House dinner: '*Comment allez-vous?* My wife speaks good French. I understand only one out of five words, but always *"de Gaulle"*.'

Jack Kennedy first met Jacqueline Bouvier at a dinner party at the house of mutual friends, Mr and Mrs Charles Bartlett, 'who had been shamelessly matchmaking for a year,' she said. He did not hesitate. 'I leaned across the asparagus and asked her for a date.'

At their tenth wedding anniversary celebration, Jack Kennedy's present to his wife was a letter from J. J. Klejman, the New York antiques dealer, listing all the most unique antiques he had in stock, with a description and a price for each, none less than $1,000. Jackie could have any one she wanted, he said. JFK read aloud to the crowd of assembled guests the descriptions, but not the prices of these items. However, as he read the descriptions of the most expensive ones he would whisper aside, 'Got to steer her away from that one.' Ultimately, the First Lady chose a coiled serpent bracelet.

On his last trip with Jacqueline, in Fort Worth, President Kennedy paid his wife one of his final compliments. 'I appreciate you being here this morning,' he told a Fort Worth audience. 'Mrs Kennedy is organizing herself. It takes her longer, but of course she looks better than we do when she does it.'

'My brother Bob doesn't want to be in government – he promised Dad he'd go straight.'
    (JFK on his brother, Robert F. Kennedy, who was assassinated in 1968 while standing as a candidate for the Democratic presidential nomination.)

After his younger brother was appointed to serve as JFK's campaign manager, there was head-shaking amongst senior members of the President's entourage, who considered Robert Kennedy, at thirty-four, too young for the job. JFK had this to say to a group of worried Democratic leaders prior to the 1960 election: 'If I need somebody older, there's no need to go outside of the family. I can always get my Father.'

'I want you to meet my sister, Patricia Lawford, from California. Somebody asked her last week if I was her kid brother, so she knew it was time this campaign came to an end.'

(Manchester, New Hampshire,
7 November 1960)

Asked by his friend Ben Bradlee how he intended to make the sensitive announcement of nominating Robert as Attorney General, JFK replied: 'Well, I think I'll open the front door of the Georgetown house some morning about 2 A.M., look up and down the street, and if there's no one there, I'll whisper, "It's Bobby."'

Again on the subject of his brother's supposed youth and inexperience, JFK quipped: 'I see nothing wrong with giving Robert some legal experience as Attorney General before he goes out to practice law.'

(Alfa Club, Washington, DC,
21 January 1961)

*

Just before the formal statement to the press, JFK turned to Robert Kennedy and said: 'Damn it, Bobby, comb your hair and don't smile so much. They'll think we are happy about the announcement.'

'Speaking of jobs for relatives,' JFK remarked, when opinion was still buzzing about his appointment of his brother as Attorney General, 'Master Robert Kennedy, who is four, came to see me today, but I told him we already had an Attorney General.'

As Attorney General, Robert Kennedy caused controversy in Texas when he suggested that the war with Mexico had been a deplorable episode in American history. Soon after making that remark, he was asked if he had anything further to say about the Mexican war. He replied that he had discussed the matter with the President and that the latter had said he 'wasn't going to muzzle me' – but that in future all speeches on Texas should be cleared with the Vice President.

(4 March 1962)

Robert Kennedy turned out to be one of the most dynamic Attorney Generals in modern American history. A few days after a national magazine called Robert Kennedy 'the man with the greatest influence at the White House', the President received a call from his Attorney General. JFK turned to a guest as he put his hand over the mouthpiece and said, 'This is the second most powerful man in the nation calling.'

Impressed by Robert Kennedy's racket-busting style, a prominent lawyer wrote to President Kennedy that Robert would make a better Chief Executive. 'I have consulted Bobby about it,' JFK wrote back, 'and, to my dismay, the idea appeals to him.'

✳

'On this matter of experience, I had announced earlier this year that if successful I would not consider campaign contributions as a substitute for experience in appointing Ambassadors. Ever since I made that statement I have not received a single cent from my Father.'

(Alfred E. Smith Memorial Dinner,
New York City, 19 October 1960)

✳

JFK's formidable father, Joseph, frequently inspired shafts of wit such as the following, made at a fund-raising dinner in Washington: 'I have just received the following telegram from my generous Daddy. It says, "Dear Jack. Don't buy a single vote more than is necessary. I'll be damned if I'm going to pay for a landslide."'

(Gridiron dinner,
Washington, DC. 1958)

JFK liked to tell stories about what a tough business-man his father was. When one of his sisters was married, a newspaper reported that someone in Joseph Kennedy's office had acknowleged, 'with a smile' that the cost of the wedding was in the six-figure category. 'Now I know that story is a phony,' scoffed JFK. 'No one in my father's office ever smiles.'

✻

One night Joseph Kennedy presided over a Kennedy family gathering. He held forth about the family finances. 'I don't know what is going to happen to this family when I die . . .' he remonstrated. 'No one appears to have the slightest concern for how much they spend. I don't know what is going to happen to you after I am gone.'

He turned to one of his daughters and repri-manded her so severely that she rushed out of the room in tears. When she returned, Jack Kennedy glanced up and said, 'Well, don't worry. We've come to the conclusion that the only solution is to have Dad work harder.'

They all laughed at that, even Joseph Kennedy.

'In the last campaign most of the members of this luncheon group today supported my opponent – except for a very few who were under the impression that I was my father's son.'

(National Association of Manufacturers, 6 December 1961)

Elephants (the Republican party mascot) are another recurring source of Kennedy witticisms. After a trip to India, JFK was heard to remark: 'I know my Republican friends were glad to see my wife feeding an elephant in India. She gave him sugar and nuts. But of course, the elephant wasn't satisfied.'

In a campaign speech he made this off-the-cuff remark, concerning the gift of a toy donkey (the Democratic mascot) by two of his supporters: 'I have been presented with this donkey by two young ladies down there for my daughter. My daughter has the greatest collection of donkeys. She doesn't even know what an elephant looks like. We are going to protect her from that knowledge.'

(Miami, Florida, 18 October 1960)

At a dinner, JFK remarked, referring to his sister-in-law, Princess Radziwill: 'It is not true that we're going to change the name of Lafayette Square to Radziwill Square – at least not during my first term.'

In another speech, giving reference to his attempts to get Americans to drink milk, he cast a sidelight on his family life: 'I am certainly enjoying being with you newsmen this evening. None of you know how tough it is to have to drink milk three times a day.'

(Washington, DC, February 1962)

'I come here to Florida today where my family has lived for thirty years, where they have already voted for one of the two candidates, and I feel it looks pretty good to get at least two votes in Florida.'

(Miami, Florida, 18 October 1960)

'This has been my home; and God willing, wherever I serve, this shall remain my home. It was here my grandparents were born – it is here I hope my grand-children will be born.'

(Speech to Massachusetts legislature,
9 January 1961)

'I want to express my great appreciation at the opportunity to be here with you and to express my thanks to all of you for having attended this [Youth Fitness] conference. I asked those members of the Cabinet who felt they were physically fit to come here today, and I am delighted that Mr Udall and Mr Robert Kennedy and Governor Ribicoff responded to the challenge.'

(20 November 1962)

✳

'My sister, Eunice, Mrs Sargent Shriver . . . lives in Illinois. One of my sisters is married to someone who lives in New York, one in California. We realized long ago we have to carry New York, Illinois and California.'

(Elgin, Illinois, 25 October 1960)

✳

'I got a telegram tonight which said, "In honour of your birthday, I believe that you should get a rise in pay.
    Signed, Roger*
    P.S. My birthday is next month."'

(New York's Birthday Salute to President Kennedy, Madison Square Gardens, 19 May 1962)

---

* (Roger Blough, President of United States Steel)

QUESTION: 'Mr President, the people of Florida are hoping that you will again spend Christmas with them. Can you tell us what your present plans are, sir?'

PRESIDENT KENNEDY: 'My mother and father are going to Florida in December, and my wife and children hope to be there for Christmas, and if my situation permits, I will go at Christmas. If the question is the result of some stories that the tourist business in Florida is off because of our difficulties, I do not think it will be.'

(20 November 1962)

'I would like to recall a speech which Franklin Roosevelt made . . . He said, "These Republican leaders have not been content with attacks on me, or my wife or my brothers, no, not content with that, they now include my little girl's pony, Macaroni. Well, I don't resent such attacks but Macaroni does."'
(New York's Birthday Salute to President Kennedy, Madison Square Gardens, 19 May 1962)

A friend, comparing common backgrounds with Jack Kennedy, including Choate prep school, concluded that they were very much alike and said so.

'You're not at all like me,' said JFK. 'You walk like a duck.'

President Kennedy sent Dave Powers, his special assistant and close friend, with whom he swam daily in the White House pool, a scroll in recognition of his fiftieth birthday: 'President's Special Award, Physical Fitness Program. Walking fifty miles per month from TV to refrigerator and back. Presented to Dave Powers on his fiftieth birthday. In recognition of your athletic ability in hiking to my ice-box to drink my Heinekens.'

At a dinner party in 1963, JFK told friends that tax laws favoured the wealthy. He pointed out that J. Paul Getty, reputedly the richest man in the world, had paid exactly $500 in taxes the previous year, and H. L. Hunt, the Texas oil tycoon, had paid only $22,000.

When Benjamin Bradlee pointed out that that was what he and his wife had paid in 1962, JFK shook his head and said, 'The tax laws really screw people in your bracket, buddy boy.'

Laughter was important to John F. Kennedy. To a friend, he gave the gift of a silver beer mug with this inscription:

> *There are things which are real:*
> *God, human folly and laughter.*
> *The first two are beyond our comprehension*
> *So we must do what we can with the third.*

JFK loved to tell stories to children. His daughter, Caroline, was his most attentive listener. One day, while they were sitting on the stern of their boat, the *Honey Fitz*, JFK began to tell a story about a huge white whale that lived in the ocean.

Sitting on the stern next to the President, sunning himself, was a shoeless Franklin Roosevelt Jr, wearing an old, dirty pair of sweat socks.

The President continued telling his whale story to Caroline, explaining that one of the favourite delicacies for this whale was 'old, dirty sweat socks'.

Suddenly he reached over and snatched a sock off Roosevelt Jr's foot and threw it in the Atlantic.

Franklin Roosevelt Jr was slightly shocked and stared at the President, who went on to say that the only thing this strange whale liked better than one 'old, dirty sweat sock' was two – whereupon JFK reached over and grabbed the second sock and threw it overboard.

As a joke, Jackie Kennedy had one of their daughter's finger-paintings – a gaudy design of red, yellow and blue blobs – framed, before presenting it to the President as the latest effort by their artist friend, Bill Walton. JFK did not flinch when his wife said she had paid $600 for this work, but seemed puzzled by the 'abstract' direction Walton seemed to have taken. When Jackie confessed that the artist was in fact the infant Caroline Kennedy, JFK shrugged and said, 'Pretty good colour.'

During the hard-fought and crucial West Virginia primary, JFK's youngest brother, Ted, gave an enthusiastic speech in which he said, 'Do you want a man who will give the country leadership? Do you want a man who has vigour and vision?' When the presidential candidate took the microphone from his brother, he opened his remarks by saying: 'I would like to tell my brother that you cannot be elected president until you are thirty-five years of age.'

In the 1962 Massachusetts Senate race, Ted Kennedy defeated House Speaker John McCormack's nephew, Eddie. Adapting the familiar 'Rather Red than Dead' antithesis, JFK remarked: 'All I can say is I'd rather be Ted than Ed.'

JFK took exception to an article in the June 1962 issue of *Time*, which described his brother Ted as smiling 'sardonically'. 'Bobby and I smile sardonically,' declared the President. 'Ted will learn how to smile sardonically in two or three years, but he doesn't know how yet.'

When Edward Kennedy was elected Senator for Massachusetts in 1962, the President told a gathering of Democrats in Harrisburg, Pennsylvania: 'I should introduce myself. I am Ted Kennedy's brother.'

'Caroline's very bright,' Joseph Kennedy once commented on his granddaughter to JFK, 'smarter than you were, Jack, at that age.'

'Yes, she is,' JFK agreed. 'But look who *she* has for a father.'

The Kennedy parents did not realize that Caroline could read until one night when Jack Kennedy, still a senator campaigning for the presidency, was in the bath at the couple's Georgetown house. Caroline burst in and threw a copy of *Newsweek* with her father on the cover into the tub, shouting gleefully, 'Daddy!'

After his nomination as presidential candidate in the summer of 1960, JFK made his nightly call to his young daughter Caroline, only to be told by her nurse, Maud Shaw, that she was not yet returned from a friend's birthday party. JFK sighed and said to Miss Shaw, 'She's got to start staying home at night.'

Shown a picture of a newborn nephew in August 1963, JFK remarked laconically, 'He looks like a fine baby – we'll know more later.'

During the presidential campaign, Caroline became a favourite of the White House press corps. She frequently engaged in repartee with the reporters. When a congressman told her father that Caroline had informed him that she didn't want to live in the White House, JFK was sceptical. 'That's not my problem with Caroline,' he said. 'My problem is to keep her from holding press conferences.'

Asked if he hoped the expectant Mrs Kennedy would have a baby boy in 1960, JFK smiled. 'I have a daughter and I know it sounds terrible and treasonous, but I really don't mind having another daughter again if that is the way it goes.'

After the assassination of President Kennedy, his young son John Jr, asked William Haddad, an associate of JFK's, 'Are you a daddy?' Haddad admitted that he was. Little John Jr said, 'Then will you throw me up in the air?'

One day the First Lady asked the President what kind of day it was. JFK shook his head regretfully and listed ten things that had gone wrong that morning. He flashed a grin: 'And the day is only half over.'

A photograph of two-year-old John Kennedy Jr, racing towards his father, to be caught up and tossed in his arms, captured the heart of the American people at the height of 'Camelot' fervour. Taken as the President got off Air Force One and walked towards his waiting family, the photograph was widely reproduced. When JFK saw the picture on a front page he smiled and said, 'Every mother in the United States is saying, "Isn't it wonderful to see that love between a son and his father, the way that John races to be with his father." Little do they know that that son would have raced right by his father to get to the helicopter, but his dad stepped into his path and grabbed him.'

'The White House was designed by James Hoban, a noted Irish-American architect,' said President Kennedy, in addressing the Irish parliament in Dublin on 28 June 1962, 'and I have no doubt that he believed by incorporating several features of the Dublin style he would make it more homelike for any president of Irish descent. It was a long wait, but I appreciate his efforts. There is also an unconfirmed rumour that Hoban was never fully paid for his work on the White House. If this proves to be true, I will speak to our Secretary of State about it.'

Jack and Jacqueline Kennedy sometimes quarrelled, and as with many married couples, these disputes were often about money. Once, furious that his wife had spent nearly $150,000 in a year at department stores, JFK exclaimed, 'She thinks she can go on spending forever. I don't understand what the hell she's doing with all those things. God, she's driving me crazy!' He then turned to an aide and asked, 'Is there a Spenders Anonymous?'

During the Cuban missile crisis, the President noticed his daughter, Caroline, running across the White House lawn. 'Caroline,' JFK shouted, 'have you been eating candy?' Caroline did not answer. 'Caroline,' repeated the President, 'have you been eating candy? Answer yes, no, or maybe.'

On one of his last weekends, in November 1963, the President and First Lady visited their newly constructed home in Virginia. JFK was photographed by the visiting White House reporter feeding lumps of sugar to his pet pony. When the sugar lumps were all gone, the pony began nibbling on the President. 'Keep shooting,' JFK instructed the photographer. 'You're about to watch a president being eaten by a horse.'

During a trip to Ireland, President Kennedy visited his third cousin Mary Ryan, who prepared a sumptuous buffet in his honour. 'I want to thank all of those who prepared this,' said JFK. 'It was a great effort on their part. We can promise we will come only once every ten years.'

'It is my pleasure to be back from whence I came,' announced President Kennedy on his arrival in Wexford, Ireland, on 28 June 1963. 'Many people are under the impression that all the Kennedys are in Washington, but I am happy to see so many present who have missed the boat.'

Visiting Cork on the same trip, JFK quipped, 'I don't want to given the impression that every member of this administration is Irish. It just seems that way.'

JFK then fondly recalled his Irish ancestors. 'When my great-grandfather left here to become a cooper in east Boston, he carried nothing with him except two things, a strong religious faith and a strong desire for liberty. And I'm glad to say that all of his great-grandchildren have valued that inheritance. If he hadn't left, I'd have been working over at the Albatross company.'

On the same trip to Ireland, JFK introduced a friend to the crowd: 'And now I would like to introduce to you the pastor at the church which I go to, who comes from Cork – Monsignor O'Mohoney. He is the pastor of a poor, humble flock in Palm Beach, Florida.'

✳

'You're yelling for that damn ball to go in the hole and I'm watching a promising political career coming to an end!' Jack Kennedy spoke calmly to his excited golf partner in a game played late in the 1960 presidential campaign.

On a short hole, Jack hit a nearly perfect shot; it landed on the green and rolled straight for the flag – almost a hole-in-one.

'If that ball had gone into that hole,' JFK said with a sigh of mock relief, 'in less than an hour the word would be out to the nation that another golfer was trying to get into the White House.'

He glanced up at a small crowd of onlookers. 'If that group of people hadn't been watching from the road I wonder what it would have cost me to have our two trusted caddies keep quiet until after the convention.'

Jack Kennedy was playing a round of golf with Jackie. The couple had reached the seventeenth hole at the Hyannis Port golf club, and Jackie was having trouble getting out of the sand-trap. The ball kept trickling back down into the trap. After she had taken many swings at it, JFK lost patience. Taking the club from his wife, he said: 'Let me show you.' After a few practice swings, he brought the club back gracefully and swung mightily. The ball rose a couple of inches and trickled back into the sand. Unperturbed by this loss of face, JFK handed the golf club back to Jackie. 'See,' he said. 'That's how you do it.'

JFK, the 'fashion-plate' President, had a penchant for expensive clothes, usually conservative in design and always immaculate. He changed frequently, and was intimately familiar with his large wardrobe.

One night Ted Sorenson needed a necktie, and Dave Powers swiped one from the President's closet that he was sure JFK never wore.

JFK's first words as he stepped into the room were, 'Is that my tie you're wearing?'

On another occasion, the fashion-conscious President was asked by a bold reporter how many times he had changed his shirt that day.

'Four,' replied JFK.

Pressed for details, he explained that he had started out with a clean shirt, put on another after his swim before his lunch honouring the Bolivian president, donned a third after the lunch because it had been so hot during the lunch, and he changed into his fourth clean shirt after a bath before dinner.

In an interview shortly after he became president, JFK was asked: 'Mr President, it has been a long time since a president and his family have been subjected to such a heavy barrage of teasing and fun-poking and satire. There have been books on 'Backstairs at the White House' and cartoon books with clever sayings and photo albums with [speech] balloons, and now there is a smash hit record. Can you tell us whether you read them and listened to them and whether they produced annoyment or enjoyment?'

To which the President deftly replied, 'Annoyment. Yes, I have read them and listened to Mr Meader's record, but I thought it sounded more like Teddy than it did me, so he's annoyed.'

In April 1961, after President Kennedy had nominated John Galbraith as the new United States Ambassador to India, Mr Kennedy was informed by Mr Galbraith that the Ambassador-to-be's young son, Peter, was not too anxious to leave all his friends in Boston and move to India. The President sent the following soothing letter to young Peter Galbraith:

Dear Peter

I learned from your father that you are not anxious to give up your school and friends for India. I think I know a little bit about how you feel.

More than twenty years ago, our family was similarly uprooted when we went to London where my father was Ambassador.

My younger brother and sisters were about your age. They had, like you, to exchange new friends for old.

For anyone interested, as your father says you are, in animals, India has the most fascinating possibilities. The range is from elephants to cobras, although I gather the cobras have to be handled professionally.

As a P.S. the President added: I wish a little I were going also.

'I haven't read all of Mr Lasky. I've just gotten the flavour of it,' JFK replied, asked to comment on a book by Victor Lasky, which was highly critical of him. 'I see it's been highly praised by Mr Drummond, Mr Krock, and others. I'm looking forward to reading it, because the part that I read was not so brilliant as I gather the rest of it is from what they say about it.'

Reportedly the President was said to have an aversion to hats. However, one day JFK was spotted carrying a felt hat in Newport in 1963 – not wearing it, carrying it.

'I've got to carry one for a while,' he explained sheepishly. 'They tell me I'm killing the industry.'

Education, Arts and Letters

When President Kennedy asked Professor James Toibin of Yale University to come to Washington as a member of his Council of Economic Advisors, Toibin told the President, 'I'm just an Ivory Tower economist.'

'That's the best kind,' replied JFK. 'As a matter of fact, I'm an Ivory Tower president.'

Reading a CIA report, presidential aide Major General Chester Clifton came across the word *draconian*. Puzzled by its meaning, he looked it up and wrote in the margin 'Cruel, inhuman!'

When President Kennedy read the report, he noticed the marginalia. 'Who put this here?' he asked.

'I did,' Clifton answered.

'That's the trouble with you military,' said JFK. 'Now if you'd had a classic Harvard education, you would have known what the word meant.'

A few days later, JFK was reading another CIA report and stumbed across a technical military term, *permissive link*. Kennedy asked Clifton, 'What's this mean?'

Clifton explained it, adding, 'Mr President, if you'd had a classic military education at West Point, you would have known what the term meant.'

The President laughed and said to Clifton, 'Touché.'

'I would like to announce at this time that as Commander-in-Chief, I am exercising my privilege of directing the Secretary of the Army and the Superintendent of West Point to remit all existing confinements and other cadet punishments and I hope it will be possible to carry this out today.

General Westmoreland was slightly pained to hear that this was impending in view of the fact that one cadet, who I am confident will some day be head of the Army, had just been committed for eight months and is about to be released. But I am glad to have this opportunity to participate in the advancement of his military career.

I want to say that I wish all of you the greatest success. While I say that, I am not unmindful of the fact that two graduates of this Academy have reached the White House and neither was a member of my party. Until I'm more certain that this trend will be broken, I wish that all of you may be generals and not Commanders-in-Chief.'

(West Point Commencement Address,
7 June 1962)

'What freedom alone can bring is the liberation of the human mind and spirit which finds its greatest flowering in the free society.'

(On the National Culture Center,
29 November 1962)

'I feel honoured to join you at this distinguished university. In the year 1717, King George I of England donated a very valuable library to Cambridge University and at very nearly the same time, had occasion to dispatch a regiment to Oxford.

The King, remarked one famous wit, had judiciously observed the condition of both universities – one was a learned body in need of loyalty and the other was a loyal body in need of learning.

I am deeply honoured by the degree which you awarded me today and I think it is appropriate to speak at this university noted for both loyalty and learning.'

(University of Maine, 19 October 1963)

'The last time that I came to this stadium was twenty-two years ago, when I visited it in November of 1940 as a student at a near-by small school for the game with Stanford. I must say, I had a much warmer reception today than I did on that occasion. In those days, we used to fill these universities for football, and now we do it for academic events, and I'm not sure that this doesn't represent a rather dangerous trend for the future of our country.'

(University of California, 23 March 1962)

'I appreciate your president having made me an honorary visiting professor, and I will assure you that my first lecture will be very brief.'

> (Address to students at Rice University,
> Houston, Texas, 12 September 1962)

'Nothing beats brains,' replied President Kennedy when asked his opinion of McGeorge Bundy, his Special Assistant for National Security Affairs.

JFK liked to tell the story of Charles R. Cherington, a Harvard professor critical of Bundy when 'Mac' was dean of the faculty of arts and sciences at Harvard and Cherington was teaching government. The government professor, in one of his classes, referred to Bundy as a 'son of a bitch'. In his next lecture, Cherington informed his students that one of them had apparently reported his remark to Bundy, who had then summoned Cherington to his office. There, Cherington said, he apologized to Bundy for calling him a son of a bitch, and Bundy apologized to him for being one.

'Our nation's first great leaders were also our first great scholars.'

> (University of North Carolina,
> Chapel Hill, 12 October 1962)

Greeting students who had been learning about government as participants in the Senate youth programme, on 1 February 1963, President Kennedy expressed the hope that one of the young men in the group would one day occupy the White House – but not right away . . .

'Sometimes I wish I just had a summer job here.'
  (To students working in Washington, 21 June 1962)

'I want to express my appreciation for becoming an instant graduate of this academy and I consider it an honour.
  I congratulate you all, and most of all, I congratulate your mothers and fathers who made it possible.'
(United States Air Force Academy,
Graduation Exercises in Colorado Springs,
5 June 1963)

Addressing students at the University of North Carolina, President Kennedy said he did not plan to adopt from the Belgian constitution a provision of giving three votes instead of one to college graduates – 'at least not until more Democrats go to college.'

Secretary of Labor, Arthur Goldberg was credited with averting a strike at the Metropolitan Opera during 1961. President Kennedy paid notice to Mr Goldberg's efforts at a Washington dinner party, where the entertainment included Metropolitan Opera stars Roberta Peters and Jerome Hines. In introducing the opera stars to the audience, the President remarked: 'The singers have appeared here under the sponsorship of Arthur Goldberg.'

(25 September 1961)

French President Charles de Gaulle announced that France had developed her own nuclear force to be independent of the United States. Soon afterwards, President Kennedy accepted a loan of Leonardo da Vinci's masterpiece, the *Mona Lisa*, from the French Minister of Culture:

'We in the United States are grateful for this loan from the leading artistic power in the world, France. I must note further that this painting has been kept under careful French control. And I want to make it clear that, grateful as we are for this painting, we will continue to press ahead with the effort to develop an independent artistic force and power of our own.'

'Let me begin by expressing my appreciation for the very deep honour you have conferred upon me. As General de Gaulle occasionally acknowledges America to be the daughter of Europe, so I am pleased to come to Yale, the daughter of Harvard.

It might be said now that I have the best of both worlds: a Harvard education and a Yale degree.

I am particularly glad to become a Yale man because as I think about my troubles, I find that a lot of them have come from other Yale men. Among businessmen, I have had minor disagreement with Roger Blough of the Law School class of 1931 and I have had some complaints too from my friend, Henry Luce, of the class of 1920, not to mention, always, William F. Buckley Jr, of the class of 1950.'

(Yale Commencement Address, 11 June 1962)

Poet Robert Frost was honoured by Congress. The noted poet was presented the Congressional Medal in recognition of his contributions to American letters. In awarding the medal to Mr Frost at the White House, President Kennedy said that he supposed that the poet was disappointed that it was not a more controversial decision in voting the medal for Mr Frost but a unanimous one. The President went on to say:

'It's the only thing they've been able to agree on for a long time.'

(25 March 1961)

The Kennedy White House hosted many literary and artistic events and welcomed musicians, artists and writers to its receptions. As JFK once wryly commented: 'It's become a sort of eating place for artists. But *they* never ask *us* out.'

John Kennedy liked to quote well-known poets. One of his favourites was Robert Frost. JFK once concluded a speech at New York University with these lines from one of Frost's most famous poems: 'But I have promises to keep . . . And miles to go before I sleep . . . And miles to go before I sleep.' He paused for effect and then added: 'And now I go to Brooklyn.'

'Great idea!' JFK responded enthusiastically, when it was suggested that he invite Robert Frost to speak at the Inauguration. 'But with Frost's skill with words, people will remember his speech instead of mine. I think we'd better have him read a poem.'

The President
and the Press

John F. Kennedy was an adept and witty performer at press conferences, as well as when making formal speeches. The following is a sample of his quick-wittedness when confronted with awkward questions from the press.

QUESTION: 'There have been published reports that some high-placed Republican people have been making overtures to your Secretary of Defense for him to be their 1968 candidate for president. If you thought that Mr McNamara were seriously considering these overtures, would you continue him in your cabinet?'

PRESIDENT KENNEDY: 'I have too high a regard for him to launch his candidacy yet.'

(25 January 1963)

QUESTION: 'Mr President, now that the United States is being transmitted instantaneously overseas via Telstar, do you think the US networks should make a greater effort to do something about the "vast wasteland"?'

PRESIDENT KENNEDY: 'I'm going to leave Mr Minow* to argue the wasteland issue, I think.'

(24 July 1962)

* (Newton Minow was the chairman of the Federal Communication Committee [FCC], 1961–3)

QUESTION: 'Mr President, you have said, and I think more than once, that heads of government should not go to the summit to negotiate agreements but only to approve agreements negotiated at a lower level. Now it's being said and written that you're going to eat those words and go to a summit without any agreement at a lower level. Has your position changed, sir?'

PRESIDENT KENNEDY: 'Well, I'm going to have a dinner for all the people who've written it and we'll see who eats what.'

(7 March 1962)

After eighteen months as US President, Jack Kennedy was asked to comment on the press treatment of his administration thus far:

'Well, I'm reading more and enjoying it less.'

(9 May 1962)

John Kennedy was surprised to receive the endorsement of *The New York Times*, which usually supported Republicans. Once elected, the President testified: 'In part, at least, I am one person who can truthfully say, "I got my job through *The New York Times*."'

QUESTION: 'Mr President, some time ago you said that you were reading more now but enjoying it less. Do you have any more current observations on American journalism or on your personal reading habits?'

PRESIDENT KENNEDY: No, I want to say that I am looking forward to all of you coming to see the White House this afternoon between six and seven. Mr Arthur Krock wrote of the temptations and seductions which take place in the press in the White House. But I want you to know that we expect that you will all emerge with your journalistic integrity and virtue unmarred. You will be courteous to the host on all occasions but it is not necessary that your views be changed.

(American Society of Newspaper Editors,
Washington, DC, 19 April 1963)

QUESTION: 'Mr President, the Republican National Committee recently adopted a resolution saying you were pretty much of a failure. How do you feel about that?'

PRESIDENT KENNEDY: 'I assume it passed unanimously.'

(17 July 1963)

QUESTION: 'Mr President, Senator Margaret Chase Smith has proposed that a watchdog committee be created. What is your reaction?'

PRESIDENT KENNEDY: 'To watch Congressmen and Senators? Well, that will be fine if they feel they should be watched.'

(21 March 1963)

'What we need most of all is a constant flow of new ideas – a government and a nation and a press and a public opinion which respect new ideas and respect the people who have them.'

(John F. Kennedy,
Strategy of Peace, 1960)

On a state visit to France, President Kennedy attended the Paris ballet one night, as a guest of President Charles de Gaulle. During the intermission, the Kennedys and their host retired to a theatre anteroom. French photographers were allowed entry, for a quick historical portrait, then dismissed with an imperious flick of a De Gaulle finger.

'Don't you wish you could control your photographers like that?' a reporter asked President Kennedy.

JFK replied: 'You must remember that I wasn't recalled to office as *my* country's saviour.'

(1 June 1961)

'I appreciate very much your generous invitation to be here tonight.

You bear heavy responsibilities these days and an article I read some time ago reminded me of how particularly heavy the burdens of present-day events bear upon your profession.

You may remember that in 1851, the *New York Herald Tribune*, under the sponsorship of Horace Greeley, included as its London correspondent an obscure journalist by the name of Karl Marx.

We are told that the foreign correspondent, Marx, stone broke and with a family ill and undernourished, constantly appealed to Greeley and managing editor Charles Dana for an increase in his munificent salary of $5 per instalment, a salary which he and Engels labelled as the 'lousiest petty bourgeois cheating'.

But when all his financial appeals were refused, Marx looked around for other means of livelihood and fame, and eventually terminated his relationship with the *Tribune* and devoted his talents full time to the cause that would bequeath to the world the seeds of Leninism, Stalinism, revolution and the Cold War.

If only this capitalistic New York newspaper had treated him more kindly, if only Marx had remained a foreign correspondent, history might have been different, and I hope all publishers will bear this lesson in mind the next time they receive a poverty-stricken appeal for a small increase in the expense account from an obscure newspaperman . . .'

(Address to American Newspaper Publishers Association, 27 April 1961)

'I have selected as the title of my remarks tonight, "The President and the Press". Some may suggest that this would be more naturally worded "The President vs the Press", but these are not my sentiments tonight. It is true, however, that when a well-known diplomat from another country demanded recently that our State Department repudiate certain newspaper attacks on his colleague, it was necessary for us to reply that this administration was not responsible for the press, for the press had already made it clear that it was not responsible for this administration.

If, in the last few months, your White House reporters and photographers have been attending church services with regularity, that has surely done them no harm. On the other hand, I realize that your staff and wire service photographers may be complaining that they do not enjoy the same green privileges at the local golf courses which they once did. It is true that my predecessor did not object as I do to pictures of one's golfing skill in action. But neither, on the other hand, did he ever bean a Secret Service man.'

(ibid.)

'Karl Marx used to write for the *Herald Tribune*, but that isn't why I cancelled my subscription.'

(18 November 1962)

'To paraphrase the old saying, "Good news is no news."'

(JFK on the press)

President Kennedy resigned his Metropolitan Club membership as a gesture of disapproval of the exclusive Washington club's refusal to admit African-Americans. However, the President refused Moise Tshombe, the rebel Congolese leader, a US entry visa. Arthur Krock of *The New York Times*, who remained a member of the Metropolitan Club, took up Tshombe's cause with President Kennedy.

JFK cut off Krock with this: 'Arthur, I'll give Tshombe a visa if you'll take him to lunch at the Metropolitan Club.'

Being interviewed by a *Look* magazine reporter, John F. Kennedy was asked about a particularly vicious rumour in private circulation. 'You print that story,' he said, 'and I just might end up owning *Look* magazine.'

At a press conference the President was asked by a reporter: 'This being Valentine's Day, sir, do you think it might be a good idea if you would call Senator Strom Thurmond of South Carolina down to the White House for a heart-to-heart talk over what he calls your defeatist foreign policy?'

'Well,' replied President Kennedy, 'I think that that meeting should probably be presented at a lower level.'

JFK
on Women

Renowned in his private life as an incorrigible ladies'
man – his glamorous partners are said to have included
screen goddess Marilyn Monroe (who famously sang
'Happy Birthday' to him at a Madison Square Gardens
celebration) – JFK was in public a defender of women's
rights, and ahead of his time in promoting the cause of
equal pay for women.

'I gave everything a good deal of thought,' Jack Kennedy wrote to his friend Paul Fay Jr in July 1953, 'so am getting married this fall. This means the end of a promising political career as it has been based up to now almost completely on the old sex appeal.'

John Kennedy attributed much of his success in politics to women voters. When running for the Senate in 1952, the 'tea party' was a favourite Kennedy campaign fund-raiser. 'In the first place, for some strange reason there are more women than men in Massachusetts, and they live longer. Secondly, my grandfather, the late John F. Fitzgerald, ran for the United States Senate thirty-six years ago against my opponent's grandfather, Henry Cabot Lodge, and he lost by only 30,000 votes in an election where woman were not allowed to vote. I hope that by impressing the female electorate I can more than take up the slack.'

'When I came to Washington to the US Senate, I brought a number of young ladies from Massachusetts to be secretaries. They all got married. Then I got a whole new set of girls and they got married. So if any of you girls feel the prospects are limited in this community, you come and work for me.'

'Looking at all you ladies and seeing what you have done with some of your distinguished officeholders,' JFK observed at a Democratic women's breakfast, 'I recall an experience of the suffragettes who picketed the White House back during the First World War. The leader of the suffragettes was arrested. And as she was taken away in a truck, she turned to her girls and said, "Don't worry, girls. Pray to the Lord. *She* will protect you."'

'Women are entitled to equality of opportunity for employment in government and in industry. But a mere statement supporting equality of opportunity must be implemented by affirmative steps to see that the doors are really open for training, selection, advancement, and equal pay.'

(Creation of President's Commission on the Status of Women, Washington, DC, 14 December 1961)

Eight girls at the Dalton School in New York, inspired by Kennedy's inaugural address and a teacher's comparison of the Kennedy oratorial style to that of the great Roman orator, Cicero, collaborated on a Latin translation of the speech. They sent it to the White House and were astonished to receive a reply from the President, written entirely in Latin, thanking them for their translation. It began: 'Johannes Filiugeraldi Kennediensis, Respublicae Preaesidens, puellis Scholae Daltoni salutem pluraimam dicit.' (President John Fitzgerald Kennedy sends heartiest greetings to the girls of Dalton School).

'I come to ask your help,' JFK appealed at a Democratic women's luncheon in Queens. 'There's an old saying, "Never send a boy to do a man's job, send a lady."'

'I want to thank all of you for an important assignment,' President Kennedy addressed the newly appointed President's Commission on the Status of Women. 'We have established the Commission for two reasons. One is for my own self-protection: every two or three weeks Mrs May Craig* asks me what I am doing for women!'

* (Mrs May Craig was a member of the Women's National Press Club who worked for the Portland [Maine] *Press Herald*)

'Women should not be considered a marginal group to be employed periodically, only to be denied opportunity to satisfy their needs and aspirations when unemployment rises or a war ends.'

(Creation of President's Commission on the Status of Women, Washington, DC, 14 December 1961)

'Women have basic rights which should be respected and fostered as part of our nation's commitment to human dignity, freedom, and democracy.'

(ibid.)

The President made this response to a group of women delegates to the United Nations, who had suggested at a White House function that someday there might be a woman president: 'I want to say that I had not expected that the standard of revolt would be raised in the Royal Pavilion here, but I'm always rather nervous about how you talk about women who are active in politics, whether they want to be talked about as women or as politicians.'

The Cold War

The intense and often bitter political rivalry with the Soviet Union – which became known as the 'Cold War' – was a legacy JFK inherited from his predecessors Dwight D. Eisenhower and Harry S. Truman. The latter's presidency has become identified with the anti-Communist hysteria of the McCarthyite era, and although this was never as intense during Kennedy's administration, JFK was at times an enthusiastic 'cold warrior'. Nikita Khrushchev, the Soviet Premier, was Kennedy's opposite number at the Kremlin; he and JFK maintained a respectful, if wary, relationship during the years of Kennedy's incumbency, sparring amicably over which of the two superpowers would be the first to put a man into space, and – less amicably – over Cuba.

When President Kennedy first met with Soviet leader Nikita Khrushchev in Vienna for foreign policy talks, Khrushchev tried to claim some credit for Kennedy's victory over Nixon.

Khrushchev explained if he had released Francis Gary Powers (the American U-2 pilot shot down over Russia in May 1960) just before the election, Kennedy would have lost by at least 200,000 votes.

'Don't spread the story around,' JFK said, smiling. 'If you tell everybody that you like me better than Nixon, I'll be ruined at home.'

During his meeting with Premier Khrushchev in Vienna, President Kennedy noticed a medal on the Russian leader's chest and asked what it was. Premier Khrushchev replied that it was the Lenin Peace Prize.

'I hope you keep it,' commented JFK.

In the course of negotiations with Premier Khrushchev on the nuclear test ban treaty, President Kennedy quoted a Chinese proverb: 'The journey of a thousand miles begins with a one step.'

'You seem to know the Chinese very well,' Chairman Khrushchev remarked.

JFK smiled, and said prophetically, 'We may both get to know them better.'

During talks President Kennedy and Premier Khrushchev in Vienna, the discussion became heated.

'Do you ever admit a mistake?' Kennedy exclaimed.

'Certainly,' said Khrushchev. 'In a speech before the Twentieth Party Congress, I admitted all of Stalin's mistakes.'

'Those were Stalin's mistakes,' said JFK. 'Not *your* mistakes.'

'I do not hold out any magic hopes for a sudden thaw or a certain timetable.'

✳

'I know something about Mr Khrushchev, whom I met a year ago in the Senate Foreign Relations Committee, and I know something about the nature and history of his country, which I visited in 1939. Mr Khrushchev himself, it is said, told the story a few years ago about the Russian who ran through the Kremlin shouting, "Khrushchev is a fool. Khrushchev is a fool." He was sentenced, the Premier said, to twenty-three years in prison, "three for insulting the party secretary, and twenty for revealing a state secret."'

(Pikesville, Maryland,
16 September 1960)

✳

'Arms alone are not enough to keep the peace – it must be kept by men. Our instrument and hope is the United Nations – and I see little merit in the impatience of those who would abandon this imperfect world instrument because they dislike our imperfect world.'

'In the past, those who foolishly sought power by riding the back of the tiger ended up inside.'

'Experience has taught us that an agreement to negotiate does not always mean a negotiated agreement.'

Secretary of State Dean Rusk played an important role in the Vienna talks between President Kennedy and Premier Khrushchev.

One day at lunch, Rusk boasted to Khrushchev about a new kind of experimental corn that grew three feet from seed in sixty days.

Khrushchev interrupted Rusk. 'I know what's what – you told Gromyko in Geneva and he told me, but I wrote to a friend of mine in America [Roswell Garst, whose Iowa farm Khrushchev had visited during his trip to the United States] and he told me it wasn't true.'

Later Khrushchev was boasting to Kennedy about Soviet technological feats, not only in space but on the earth, including a newly developed process of making vodka out of natural gas.

President Kennedy interrupted Khrushchev, saying, 'That sounds like some of Dean Rusk's sixty-day corn to me.'

'The first test of leadership in this country is not an ability to argue with the Russians – anyone can do that. It is the ability to tell the people the truth about our danger – and to summon the people to meet it.'

President Kennedy, as a national spokesman, offered this rebuttal to Khrushchev's statement in the summer of 1961 that the United States was like a 'worn-out runner'.

'Chairman Khrushchev has compared the United States to a worn-out runner living on its past performance, and states that the Soviet Union would out-produce the United States by 1970. Without wishing to trade hyperbole with the Chairman, I do suggest that he reminds me of the tiger hunter who had picked a place on the wall to hang the tiger's skin long before he caught the tiger. The tiger has other ideas . . . In short, the United States is not such an aged runner and, to paraphrase Mr Coolidge, "We *do* choose to run."'

'Unconditional war can no longer lead to unconditional victory.'

'The hour is late – but the agenda is long.'

'You're an old country,' Premier Khrushchev told President Kennedy at their Vienna meeting on 3 June 1961. 'We're a young country.'

'If you'll look across the table,' replied the forty-four-year-old president, 'you'll see that we are not so old.'

'Mr Khrushchev may have known his Marx – but his Marx did not know the United States.'

War and Peace

Throughout his time as president, John F. Kennedy spoke often of the need for global arms control, to protect the future of the world. He was all too aware of the horrors that an all-out nuclear confrontation could bring about and, consequently, conveyed only serious views on the subject. He was able, however, to look back on his earlier Second World War experiences with a certain degree of humour.

During the Second World War, Jack Kennedy served in the Pacific as a commissioned naval officer. In August 1943 in Blackett Strait in the Solomon Islands, a Japanese destroyer rammed the PT-109 torpedo boat he commanded and sank it.

Jack Kennedy saved the life of one wounded man by seizing the end of his life jacket in his teeth and towing him to an island three miles away.

Lieutenant Kennedy, with some colleagues, reached a nearby island but found it to be held by the Japanese. He and another officer then swam to another island, where they persuaded the inhabitants to send a message to other US forces, who rescued them. It was several days before JFK and his crew were rescued. The suffered severely from lack of food and water during that period, and Lieutenant Kennedy kept up the spirits of the survivors with his sense of humour.

When he finally heard the voice of a rescuer crying, 'Hey, Jack!' from a distance, Jack yelled back, 'Where the hell have you been?'

'We've got some food for you,' called out the rescuer.

'No thanks,' quipped Kennedy, who kept his sense of humour throughout the crisis, 'I just had a coconut.'

Shortly thereafter JFK had a run-in with a doctor. 'I went to see the Doc about some coral infections I got,' he recalled. 'He asked me how I got them – I said, "Swimming." He then burst out with, "Kennedy, you know swimming is forbidden in this area. Stay out of the goddamned water!" So now it's an official order.'

On a trip to the West Coast, President Kennedy was asked by a little boy, 'Mr President, how did you become a war hero?' To which JFK replied, 'It was absolutely involuntary. They sank my boat.'

JFK referred to his harrowing brush with death in the Pacific during the Second World War as 'an interesting experience' during a television interview with Edward R. Murrow.

'Interesting,' repeated Murrow. 'I should think that would be one of the great understatements.'

Cuban Missile Crisis

In October 1962 the Cuban Missile Crisis brought the world to the brink of nuclear war, when the United States confronted the Soviet Union over its installation of ballistic missiles in Cuba. President Kennedy demonstrated his determination to have the missiles removed, and after days of tension and mounting anxiety about the threat of nuclear conflict, Russian Premier Nikita Khrushchev eventually ordered their withdrawal.

Pierre Salinger, the President's Press Secretary, was one of the few who had a relationship with the President that allowed him to burst into the Oval Office unannounced.

'Plucky', as JFK called him, took pride in being able to trace leaks to their source.

On one occasion the President was furious when there was a leak on the Cuban embargo. He asked Salinger to spare no effort to find out who leaked it.

Salinger, a former investigative reporter, worked for two days and then reported back to the President that he had been able to trace the leak.

'Who was it?' the President asked intently.

'You,' said Salinger.

'What do you mean?' asked JFK.

'Didn't you tell George Smathers?' replied Salinger.

JFK nodded. He had told the Florida senator.

'Well, George told a friend of his on the *Tampa Tribune* and that was that,' declared Salinger.

JFK stared at Salinger, grinned and said, 'Plucky . . .'

At the height of the Cuban Missile Crisis, JFK remarked, 'I guess this is the week I earn my salary.'

JFK joked that the worse Eisenhower did as president, the more popular he became with the public. When a Gallup poll taken after the ill-fated Bay of Pigs invasion revealed that President Kennedy's own popularity was higher than ever – with an 83 per cent approval rating – he shook his head and said, 'My God, it's as bad as Eisenhower!'

'The 1930s taught us a clear lesson: aggressive conduct, if allowed to go unchecked and unchallenged, ultimately leads to war. This nation is opposed to war. We are also true to our word. Our unswerving objective, therefore, must be to prevent the use of these missiles against this or any other country, and to secure their withdrawal or elimination from the Western Hemisphere.'

(Radio and television address,
Washington, DC, 22 October 1962)

'The cost of freedom is always high – but Americans have always paid it. And one path we shall never choose, and that is the path of surrender or submission.'

(ibid.)

Encouraging
Scientific Advances:
The Space Race

During his presidency, John F. Kennedy placed a higher priority on space exploration that any president before or since. In May 1961, he fired the public imagination by announcing that the United States would fly men to the moon and back within the decade, and during his 'thousand days' in office, the United States duly caught up with and surpassed the USSR in the 'space race'. NASA's Launch Operations Center was renamed the Kennedy Space Center in his honour in December 1963.

'We have undertaken . . . a great new effort in outer space. Our aim is not simply to be first on the moon, any more than Charles Lindbergh's real aim was to be the first to Paris. His aim was to develop the techniques of our own country and other countries in the field of air and the atmosphere, and our objective in making this effort, which we hope will one day place one of our citizens on the moon, is to develop in a new frontier of science, commerce and co-operation, the position of the United States and the free world.'
(State of the Union message, 11 January 1962)

The President interrupted a press conference on 29 November 1961 to announce to the assembled reporters that the United States had successfully sent a chimpanzee into space. 'This chimpanzee who is flying in space took off at 10.08. He reports that everything is going perfectly and working well.'

The President was critical of the previous Republican administration for losing ground to the Soviets in space exploration. He remarked: 'I wonder when he [Richard Nixon] put his finger under Mr Khrushchev's nose whether he was saying, "I know you're ahead of us in rockets, Mr Khrushchev, but we are ahead of you in colour television." I would just as soon look at black and white television and be ahead of them in rockets!'

(JFK on the space race, in Pittsburgh, Pennsylvania, 10 October 1960)

'It is, I think, a source of concern to us all that the first dogs carried around in outer space were not named Rover and Fido, but instead were named Belka and Strelka,' JFK commented at a campaign stop in Muskegon, Michigan, on 5 September 1960.

Seconds later, with a reference to Vice President Nixon's dog, he added, 'It was not named Checkers, either.'

'No man can fully grasp how far and how fast we have come, but condense, if you will, the 50,000 years of man's recorded history in a time span of but half a century. Stated in these terms, we know very little about the first forty years, except that at the end of them men had learned to use the skins of animals to cover them. Then about ten years ago, under this standard, man emerged from his caves to construct other kinds of shelter. Only five years ago man learned to write and use a cart with wheels. Christianity began less than two years ago. The printing press came this year, and less than two months ago, during this whole fifty-year span of human history, the steam engine provided a new source of power. Newton explored the meaning of gravity. Last month electric lights and telephones and automobiles became available. Only last week did we develop penicillin and television and nuclear power, and now if America's new spacecraft succeeds in reaching Venus, we will have literally reached the stars before midnight tonight.'

(Address to students at Rice University, Houston, Texas, 12 September 1962)

'Many years ago, the great British explorer George Mallory, who was to die on Mount Everest, was asked why did he want to climb it. He said, "Because it is there." Well, space is there, and we're going to climb it . . .'

(ibid.)

'We have with us today the nation's number one television performer [Alan Shepard Jr], who I think on last Friday morning secured the largest rating of any morning show in recent history.

And I think it does credit to him that he is associated with such a distinguished group of Americans whom we are all glad to honour today – his companions in the flight to outer space – so I think we'll give them all a hand. They are the tanned and healthy ones; the others are Washington employees.

(Washington Ceremony honouring Astronaut
Alan Shepard Jr, 8 May 1961)

The day before his assassination, President Kennedy spoke at the dedication of the Aero-Space Medical Health Center at Brooks Air Force Base in Texas. The President quoted Frank O'Connor's statement that he and his boyhood friends would trudge across the country until they came to a seemingly insurmountable wall. Then they would throw their hats over the wall to encourage themselves to keep going on their journey.

'This nation has tossed its cap across the wall of space,' avowed President Kennedy, 'and we have no choice but to follow it.'

On John F. Kennedy

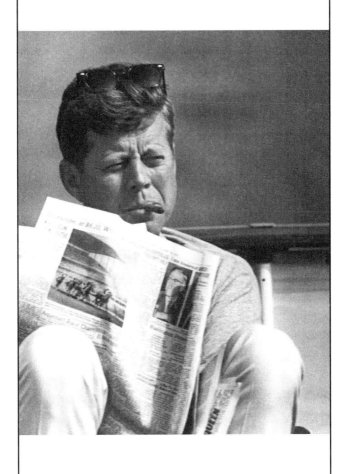

'There are moments in the cause of human freedom when his words move with a measured passion.'
(Carl Sandburg, author and poet, on John F. Kennedy, 1962)

'John Fitzgerald Kennedy . . . a great and good president, the friend of all people of goodwill; a believer in the dignity and equality of human beings; a fighter for justice; an apostle of peace.'
(Earl Warren, Chief Justice of the Supreme Court, 1963)

'We, Kennedy's godchildren, the baby-boom generation that believed his stirring words and handsome image, are like Hamlet in the first act, children of a slain leader, unaware of why he was killed or even that a false father figure inhabits the throne.'
(Oliver Stone, director, 1993)

'This is part of the fundamental dichotomy in Kennedy's character: half the "mick" politician, tough, earthy, bawdy, sentimental, and half the bright, graceful, intelligent *Playboy of the Western World* . . .'
(Benjamin Bradlee, *Conversations with Kennedy*, 1973)

'The thing about him was the extraordinary sense he gave to being alive. This makes his death so grotesque and unbelievable. No one had such vitality of personality . . .

He was life-affirming, life-enhancing. When he entered the room, the temperature changed; and he quickened the sensibilities of everyone around him.'

(Arthur Schlesinger Jr, *A Eulogy*, 1963)

'He was, perhaps, a step or two ahead of the people at times. But as an American who understood America, who brought form to its amorphous yearnings, who gave direction to its efforts, John Kennedy walked with people.'

(Senator Hubert Humphrey, 1963)

'More than any president before him, he committed the presidency to achieving full civil rights for every American. He opposed prejudice of every kind. There was no trace of meanness in this man. There was only compassion for the frailties of others. If there is a supreme lesson we can draw from the life of John F. Kennedy, it is a lesson of tolerance, a lesson of conscience, courage, and compassion.'

(Senator Abraham Ribicoff, 1963)

'His last speech on race relations was the most earnest, human and profound appeal for understanding and justice that any president has uttered since the first days of the Republic. Uniting his flair for leadership with a programme of social progress, he was at his death undergoing a transformation ...'

(Martin Luther King Jr, civil rights leader, 1963)

'So we are free to wonder, having been given not only the presidential models over the last three decades of Johnson, Nixon, Ford, Carter, Reagan, and Bush, but also the secondary examples of Humphrey, McGovern, Mondale, and Dukakis, whether any protagonist as innovative, flexible, daring, ironic, witty, and as ready to grow as Jack Kennedy ever did have a chance to change the shape of our place.'

(Norman Mailer, novelist and essayist, 1992)

'His wisdom and eloquence will undoubtedly rank with that of Jefferson, Lincoln, Wilson, and Roosevelt, men whom Kennedy himself enjoyed quoting. Future generations will surely be quoting our late president.'

(T. S. Settle, editor, 1965)